A Tramp in Berlin

New Mark Twain Stories
& an Account of Twain's Berlin Adventures
by Andreas Austilat

A Tramp in Berlin

New Mark Twain Stories

&

an Account of Twain's Berlin Adventures by Andreas Austilat

Preface by Lewis Lapham

Mark Twain
Andreas Austilat

A Tramp in Berlin

First U.S. Edition 2013 by Berlinica Publishing LLC,
255 West 43rd Street, Suite 1012, New York, New York 10036

Copyright © 2013 by Berlinica Publishing LLC

Editor: Eva C. Schweitzer
Translator: Cindy Opitz
Assistant Editor: Kristina Kalpaxis

Cover design: Jennifer Durrant at jenniferdurrantdesign.com
Cover photo: Postcard of the Brandenburg Gate, ca. 1890
Cover image retouching: Sue Yerou Imaging, Inc

Printed in the United States

All rights reserved under International and Pan-American Copyright Law. No part of this book may be used or reproduced in any manner whatsoever without written permission except in the case of brief quotations embodied in critical articles and reviews.

ISBN 978-1-935902-92-8
LCCN: 2012937894

www.berlinica.com

"Berlin is a luminous centre of intelligence—a place where the last possibilities of attaintment in all the sciences are to be had for the seeking. Berlin is a wonderful city for that sort of opportunities. They teach everything here. I don't believe there is anything in the whole earth that you can't learn in Berlin except the German language."

—*Mark Twain*

Thanks

On behalf of Berlinica, I would like to thank the people who endured endless test versions of this book, as well as everybody involved with the production of and the research for this book, namely Andy Borowitz, Jennifer Durrant, Horst Fugger, Christiane Landgrebe, Lewis Lapham, Kristina Kalpaxis, Harald Martenstein, Afriye Osei-Somuah, Denise Pangia, Cathrin Wirtz, Sue Yerou, Dan Zitin, the incredible Cindy Opitz, and, of course, the inexhaustible Andreas Austilat. I would also like to thank everybody at the Landesarchiv Berlin for their help with the pictures for the book.

My special thanks go to the Mark Twain Papers and Project at the University of Berkeley, California, especially to Vic Fischer as well as to Bob Hirst, and Neda Salem. I would also like to thank everybody whose financial contributions at Kickstarter made this book possible, namely Erika Romberg and Bob Schroeder.

Table of Contents

Foreword by Lewis Lapham   9

Mark Twain in Berlin, by Andreas Austilat   13

Stories by Mark Twain:

On Renting a Flat in Berlin   42

A Reflection on the German Stove   85
From: Conversations with Satan

Fragment of Prussian History: 107
Wilhelmina, Margravine of Bayreuth

The Chicago of Europe   132

Stories about Mark Twain:

National-Zeitung: Mark Twain in Berlin   146

Breslauer Morgenzeitung: Mark Twain   154

Berliner Tageblatt: America in Berlin   158

Sources   164

Index   168

Berlinica Presents   170

Across the Atlantic

Lewis Lapham

It was Mark Twain's gift for travel writing that first established his illuminating presence on the American literary stage. The ranking followed from the publication in 1869 of "The Innocents Abroad," Twain's account of his voyage aboard the steamship, Quaker City, bound for Europe in company with a delegation of American tourists intent upon upgrading their acquaintance with the historic past. Twain duly noted the points of interest while at the same time remarking upon the sense and sensibility of his fellow travelers as they browsed among masterpieces in Italy and France, collected intimations of immortality, and scattered stock phrases of exclamatory rapture. The book owed its success both to the author's abundant humor and to the formidable powers of observation he had acquired as a steamboat pilot on the Mississippi River to which he later attributed his angle of approach to the spectacle of the human comedy:

> "There is one faculty that the pilot must incessantly cultivate until he has brought it to absolute perfection...That faculty is memory. He cannot stop with merely thinking a thing is so and so, he must know it...one cannot easily realize what a tremendous thing it is to know every trivial detail of 1200 miles of river and know it with absolute exactness. If you will take the longest street in New York, and travel up and down it, conning its features patiently until you know every door and lamp-post and big and little sign by heart, and know them so accurately that you could instantly name the one you are abreast of when you are set down at random in that street in the middle of an inky black night, you will then have a

tolerable notion of the amount and the exactness of a pilot's knowledge who carries the Mississippi River in his head."

The exactness of Twain's perception was further refined by the sightlines of the mid-19th century American frontier, grounded in the experience that Bernard DeVoto, the historian who served as Twain's literary executor, recognized as that of a young man accustomed to scenes of human squalor and depravity, had "observed night riding and lynching and the flogging of slaves," was familiar with "commonplaces of lust and corruption," who as an apprentice printer had been "little better than a tramp," had joined the surge westward to the Nevada silver mines and the California gold camps, had there to converse "with murderers and harlots, observe a sizeable number of men die" in their boots in his immediate vicinity. A mise-en-scène in which the man who didn't see clearly didn't live long enough to hear the punch line and get the joke.

The seventy-five years of Twain's life (1835–1910) ran in parallel with America's transformation from an agrarian democracy into an industrial oligarchy. No other writer of his generation saw the country from so many vantage points or became as familiar with so many of its oddly assorted inhabitants. The turn of his mind was democratic. He held his fellow citizens in thoughtful regard not because they were rich or beautiful or famous but because they were his fellow citizens. He found them plying trades in Massachusetts, building roads in Illinois, selling patent medicines in Iowa, given to believing that across the next stretch of mountains or around the next bend in the river they would safely come home to the end of the rainbow and the pot of gold.

Twain understood America's moral code to be political, the protection of the other fellow's liberty in exchange for the protecting of one's own, the object being to provide all present with the broadest range of expression and the widest room for maneuver. The same generosity of spirit lies at or near the root of all his writing, in his travel notes and satires as in his novels and his letters. He was a man at play with the freedom of his mind, both as an author and as a popular performer on the American lecture stage. For forty years he toured the country to deliver comic monologues for dance hall girls in Carson City, to literary swells in Boston (among them Ralph Waldo Emerson and Oliver Wendell Holmes) at banquets attended by presidents Ulysses S. Grant and Theodore Roosevelt. He came to please, to produce laughter in commercial quantity and with it, "the great thing, the saving thing" that makes bearable the acquaintance of grief he knew he could ascribe to most everyone in the theater, the drawing room, or the saloon.

The blessing of Twain's humor was as gratefully received by audiences abroad as it was by those at home. He traveled forty-nine times across the Atlantic, once across the Indian Ocean and the Pacific—as a dutiful tourist admiring the rubble in the Colosseum and the sculpture in the Louvre; as itinerant sage entertaining crowds in Australia and Ceylon; as attentive bystander in London in 1897 for the pageant that was Queen Victoria's Diamond Jubilee, in Vienna in 1896 for a parading of the plumes of the Hapsburg Empire, "bodies of men-at-arms in the darling velvets of the Middle Ages . . . beautiful costumes not to be seen in this world now outside the opera and the picture-books."

During the last four years of his life, Twain composed his autobiography in the form of a deposition given to a series of stenographers while lying garrulously abed, propped up "against great snowy, white pillows" in a townhouse on lower Fifth Avenue in New York. He employs the approach that in 1859 had shaped his navigations of the Mississippi River, the flow and stream of time caught up in the net of his comprehensive and comprehending memory. The scenes of foreign pomp and circumstance serve Twain as occasions to prefer the simplicity of things American.

He does not favor the "showy episodes" of his life, choosing instead the "common experiences" that "bring the past face to face with the present," and as miscellaneous exhibits he introduces into the record, previously published anecdotes and sketches, newspaper clippings, philosophical digressions, theatrical asides, every trivial detail that he knows with the absolute exactness of a Mississippi River steamboat pilot. The result is the story of a life that is the portrait of an age, something seen in Calcutta in 1896 reminding him of something said in San Francisco in 1894, his first impression of Florence in 1892 sending him back to Missouri in 1849.

Twain brings the same gregarious and affectionate intelligence to his encounter with Kaiser Wilhelm's city of Berlin. Andreas Austilat has made of the stories, notes, and observations a joy to read and a wonder to behold.

Mark Twain in Berlin

Andreas Austilat

Berlin's Brandenburg Gate, crowned by a chariot carrying the Roman goddess Victoria, drawn by four bronze horses, leads to Pariser Platz. The historic plaza is surrounded by embassies, posh restaurants, as well as the Hotel Adlon, the Berlin Academy of the Arts and two small museums. One is devoted to the painter Max Liebermann, the other, until recently, to the Kennedys, right next to a Starbucks. The plaza was commissioned in the 1730s by Prussian King Frederick Wilhelm I; the gate was built in 1791 as a dignified entrance to the old city and Unter den Linden—then a grand road from the hunting grounds of the Tiergarten to the Berlin castle; today Berlin's main boulevard. Pariser Platz is crowded on any given day: musicians, jugglers, actors dressed as Prussian royalty, Russian soldiers, Star Wars characters, or Berlin Bears, Native Americans in full regalia, protesters of any kind in front of the American (or Russian) embassy, old-fashioned horse carriages, tour busses, and, of course, droves of tourists populate the plaza and Unter den Linden. About 120 years ago, a famous American humorist, journalist, foreign correspondent, novelist, and travel writer lived right here on Unter den Linden with a view of Pariser Platz: Samuel Langhorne Clemens, better known as Mark Twain.

"Berlin is a new city; the newest I have ever seen," marveled Twain in April 1892, in his travel letter for the *Chicago Daily Tribune* (today the *Chicago Tribune*). "The bulk of the Berlin of today has about it no suggestion of a former period. The site it stands on has traditions and a history, but the city itself has no traditions and no history . . . The main mass of the city looks as if it had been built last week . . . No other city has such an air of roominess, freedom from crowding; no other city has so many straight streets."

The Clemens family: Mark Twain (top left), his wife Olivia (top right), his daughters Susy (middle left) and Clara (middle right). Bottom photo from left to right: Clara, Olivia, Jean, Mark Twain and Susy, in 1886.

Twain and his family—his wife Olivia, his three daughters, Susy, Clara, and Jean, and his sister-in-law Susan Crane—spent half a year in the German capital, during the winter of 1891–92. At first, they stayed in a tenement in the borough of Tiergarten, a mixed neighborhood on a rather noisy street. Three months later, they moved to the much more upscale Hotel Royal on Unter den Linden, the boulevard that ran from the Brandenburg Gate to the ancient Prussian castle, a sprawling structure with an iconic green copper dome, where the emperor, Kaiser Wilhelm II lived. The area included Wilhelmstrasse, with its many Prussian ministries and banks, the Royal Friedrich Wilhelm University, city residences of aristocrats and wealthy merchants, and the Royal Library. Twain visited many of these places.

Twain was a celebrity in 1890s Berlin. He mingled with diplomats, university luminaries, princes, and princesses, and was eventually invited by the Kaiser, whom he had often watched riding down the "Holy Land," as he called the Kaiser's very own bridle path in the middle of Unter den Linden. Newspaper stories were written about Twain, and Berliners greeted him on the street. He worked on books, news articles, and travel stories; he gave speeches and he did research, on the German philosopher Arthur Schopenhauer, for instance, and on Wilhelmine of Prussia, the sister of Frederick the Great, who lived from 1709 to 1758. He translated a children's book, *Slovenly Peter,* known as *Struwwelpeter* in Germany. He also spent a lot of time managing his publishing business in America from afar. And he was not shy about having an opinion on German politics in those turbulent times.

Berlin had not been an impressive city by European standards until the middle of the 19th century. That changed rapidly in 1871, however, when Berlin became the capital, after Germany defeated France and was unified by Otto von Bismarck, the "Iron Chancellor." Bismarck governed Germany until 1890, the year he was dismissed by Kaiser Wilhelm II. In this "Gilded Age," a multitude of industrial plants, office buildings, train stations, and railroads were constructed; Germany overtook England as a mass-producer of goods. Everything was modernizing at a breathtaking speed.

Electrical street lamps were replacing the older gas lamps that had been modern only a few decades earlier. Unter den Linden had had electricity since 1888, and other streets were following suit. In 1891, the year Twain arrived, Otto Lilienthal, the "father of aviation," had succeeded in making the world's first flight on a hill in a Berlin suburb, using a hang glider he had developed himself.

The industrialization had also drawn hundreds of thousands of laborers to Berlin, many from the rural areas in the eastern German provinces of Silesia, East Prussia, West Prussia, and Pomerania. Entirely new districts had been created from scratch to house them, on former farmland. Tens of thousands of tenements, often tightly stacked and starved for light, were built on those newly drawn streets that Twain had so admired. The population of Berlin tripled, from half a million people in 1860, to one and a half million in 1890. In 1920, Berlin would have four million residents, making it the third largest city in the world, after New York and London.

So, Twain was exaggerating about the "newness" of Berlin, but only a little bit, since next to this brand new town, Chicago seemed old and venerable to him. This booming capital was the city in which Twain spent an interesting period of his life—but it is a period that has sunk into obscurity. There are only a few sources about this journey: some dozen letters written by him and to him, the handwritten diaries of Twain and his daughters Clara and Jean, a couple of newspaper stories from New York, Chicago, and also Berlin papers, and a half-dozen other people, some more, some less reliable, who chronicled that time. Even most of the stories Twain himself wrote about Berlin haven't been published until now. So, let us explore his unknown chapter of Twain's life!

The remarkable career of Samuel Langhorne Clemens began in 1853, when he left his impoverished childhood home in Hannibal, Missouri, on the banks of the Mississippi, at age eighteen (later, he would use his childhood memories in his most famous novel *The Adventures of Tom Sawyer*). He landed a printing job in St. Louis, followed by stints as a typesetter in New York and Philadelphia. At twenty, he became a river pilot for a steamboat on the Mississippi, a job he loved very much. Along his journey, he may or may not have fought briefly for the Confederacy during the Civil War. In any case, he departed for Salt Lake City soon after, tried his luck prospecting in Nevada. He also started to write for the *Territorial Enterprise* and adopted his pen name "Mark Twain," a Mississippi River term meaning "twelve feet of water." Finally, he settled in San Francisco. There, Twain began to establish a name for himself as a journalist and a travel writer, eventually visiting at least forty countries and writing about most of them.

His first trip overseas in 1867 (funded by a San Francisco newspaper) led him to the Mediterranean, France, and Palestine and resulted in the publication of the book, *The Innocents Abroad,* which was a huge success. Eleven years later, he went on his first trip to Germany, which resulted in the sequel, *A Tramp Abroad.* The book included the essay, "The Awful German Language." By then, Twain was thirty-two and traveling with Olivia, his beloved wife, whom he called "dearest Livy." She came from a progressive abolitionist family, whereas he was liberal Atheist. The couple's two daughters at the time were also on board: Susy, who was five years old, and Clara, who was three. They sailed on the *Holsatia,* a steamship run by the Hamburg–America line. On April 11, 1878, the *Holsatia* was docked at the West Side Piers in New York City, awaiting two very stormy weeks on the Atlantic Ocean.

The scene at the Manhattan piers resembled a street fair. Travelers arrived with friends and family clustering along the harbor to see them off while their luggage was loaded. The mood was only dampened by the "rain that trickled from the muddy-looking skies in a little drizzle," as *The New York Times* reported. Among the passengers was Bayard Taylor, a famous poet and translator of his time, who had just been appointed as the United States Envoy Extraordinary and Minister Plenipotentiary in Berlin. Basically, he was America's cultural ambassador to Bismarck. Taylor was accompanied by his "colored servant," according to *The Times,* while the Clemens family had a nursemaid with them. Twain and Taylor discussed what they drank in the past week—apparently a lot, according to the eavesdropping reporter. Twain, who was wearing a small black silk cap, confessed to

The Gascogne, *the ship that carried the Clemens family to France and then Berlin. Below: Bayard Taylor, the U.S. Envoy Extraordinary and Minister Plenipotentiary to Germany.*

the reporter that he was jealous of the older writer's command of the German language. Taylor, after all, had translated the quintessential German play, *Faust*. "Taylor had a large capacity for languages and a memory that was always a marvel," wrote Albert Bigelow Paine, the author of Twain's official biography in 1912. "He sang German folklore songs for them, and the 'Lorelei.'" (Sadly, Taylor would pass away only a few months later in Berlin.) Also on board was the family of Murat Halstead, a famed war correspondent who also owned a Republican newspaper (in those times, Republican were mostly known for their anti-slavery stance). Twain told the *Times* reporter that he was traveling to Germany for his health—he suffered from rheumatism—but also to be able to write in peace and quiet. "I am going to the most out-of-the-way place in Germany I can find," he said. "Fifty miles away from any railroad, where I can sleep half the time." The family would visit Heidelberg, Mannheim, Baden-Baden, and the Black Forest, as well as Switzerland and northern Italy. The trip took about two years, but they kept their mansion in Hartford, Connecticut during this time.

The Clemens family's second trip to Germany—the trip to Berlin—began in the summer of 1891. Again, the writer was accompanied not only by Olivia, but also by his now three daughters: Susy, who had turned nineteen, Clara, at the age of seventeen, and the youngest, Jean, who was eleven. Susan Crane, his wife's older, adopted sister, and one of their housemaids, Katie Leary, also went with them, though Katie would not stay in Berlin. But this voyage was completely different from their journey on the *Holsatia*, right from the get-go.

The family boarded the steamship *Gascogne* at New York's West Side Piers, which set course for the French city of Le Havre. But this time, there were no reporters at the harbor, and the trip itself resembled more of an escape than a vacation. By now, Twain was nearly bankrupt, and he desperately needed to cut down on expenses. He had invested all of his savings in a new, revolutionary printing machine, the Paige typesetter. He had hoped the technology would make him a millionaire, but the inventor, James Paige, never got the complicated contraption to work properly. Instead,

Twain lost $300,000, equivalent to nearly six million dollars today. And Twain's own publishing company, Charles Webster & Co., founded in 1884, was also facing deep financial troubles. The company had some initial success with the memoirs of President Ulysses S. Grant, which sold 350,000 copies. It also owned the rights to *Huckleberry Finn*, an eternal bestseller. But Twain had lost a lot of money on Webster's next big endeavor, the memoirs of Pope Leo VIII, which found only two hundred buyers. So this time Twain left Hartford for good, fearing that he could no longer afford his expensive household there, with its seven employees.

The basic idea was to save money by living in Europe. Also, all of Twain's previous travel books had become international bestsellers, so he was hoping for another one. In addition, he was under contract with the McClure Newspaper Syndicate, owned by Samuel Sidney McClure, which supplied dozens of newspapers in America, including the *New York Sun* and the *Chicago Daily Tribune*. For this trip, he had a commission for six lengthy "travel letters" from different locations; one of them would be from Berlin. Each of those letters would net him a thousand dollars, about $20,000 today, a huge amount for any correspondent, then and now. Therefore, the Clemens family boarded the *Gascogne* with some worries, but also with great hopes.

Aside from monetary issues, Twain ventured to Europe yet again for his deteriorating health. Now fifty-five, his rheumatism affected him to the point that he could no longer use his right arm most of the time, a catastrophe for any writer. His wife had health problems as well, having suffered from a weak heart since childhood. The couple planned to visit various European spa cities during the first, warmer months of their trip, among them Aix-Les-Bain in France, and Marienbad, a spa in the kingdom of Bohemia, which was part of Austria-Hungary then (in the Czech Republic today). The fall marked the end of the season, so they looked forward to spending the winter in the imperial capital of the newly unified Germany.

The winter in Berlin, however, was usually brutal. It consisted of long, frosty, and foggy months when the sun hardly made an appearance, even more so in those times, when hundreds of thousands of unfiltered coal furnaces blackened the already grey winter

Pariser Platz and the Brandenburg Gate (above). In 1892, the Clemens family moved into the Hotel Royal (lower left corner). Below: Unter den Linden, Berlin's main Boulevard coming from Pariser Platz.

The corner of Pohlstrasse and Körnerstrasse in the district of Tiergarten, where the Clemens family lived in number 7 for three months. That building is gone, but it looked very much like these across the street.

sky. But Twain found some solace in the tiled coal stove in his apartment. "The Berlin stove is the best that I have seen," he wrote in the winter of 1897–98, when he and his family had already moved on to Vienna, Austria. "When we kept house there several winters ago, we charged our parlor monument at 7 in the morning with a peck of cheap briquettes made of refuse coal-dust, let the fire burn half an hour, then shut up the stove and never touched it again for twenty-four hours. All day long and up to past midnight that room was perfectly comfortable."

Upon arriving in October 1891, the Clemenses moved into a tenement near Potsdamer Strasse, an avenue Twain described as "bordered on both sides by sidewalks which are themselves wider than some of the historic thoroughfares of the old European capitals." This was clearly a street of the "new Berlin" he was so excited about. The Prussian chronicler and novelist Theodor Fontane, a descendant of French Huguenots, lived in one of the bourgeois mansions that lined Potsdamer Strasse at that same time—Twain, however, never met Fontane, as far as we know—and the actress Marlene Dietrich spent part of her childhood in Potsdamer Strasse about ten years later.

During the Golden Twenties, Potsdamer Strasse was famous for its art dealers, antique stores, and publishing houses, such as Rowohlt and S. Fischer. After World War II and the construction of the Berlin Wall, the avenue became a red light district filled with gambling halls, fast food, and squatters. But today, the street is again "establishing itself as the next big art location," as *The New York Times* reported in 2011. The *Joseph Roth Diele* is one such place, an arts café named after the author from the Weimar era, along with the *Winter Garden* Variety Theatre. Half a dozen galleries and an avantgarde fashion house have moved into the former printing plant of the daily *Tagesspiegel* as well as in the adjacent mansion built for the painter Anton von Werner in 1874. Along the backside of that building runs Körnerstrasse. The Clemens family moved into an apartment at number 7 Körnerstrasse. Unfortunately, the house does not exist anymore, and there are no photos of Körnerstrasse during Twain's time there either. But the floor plan and a drawing

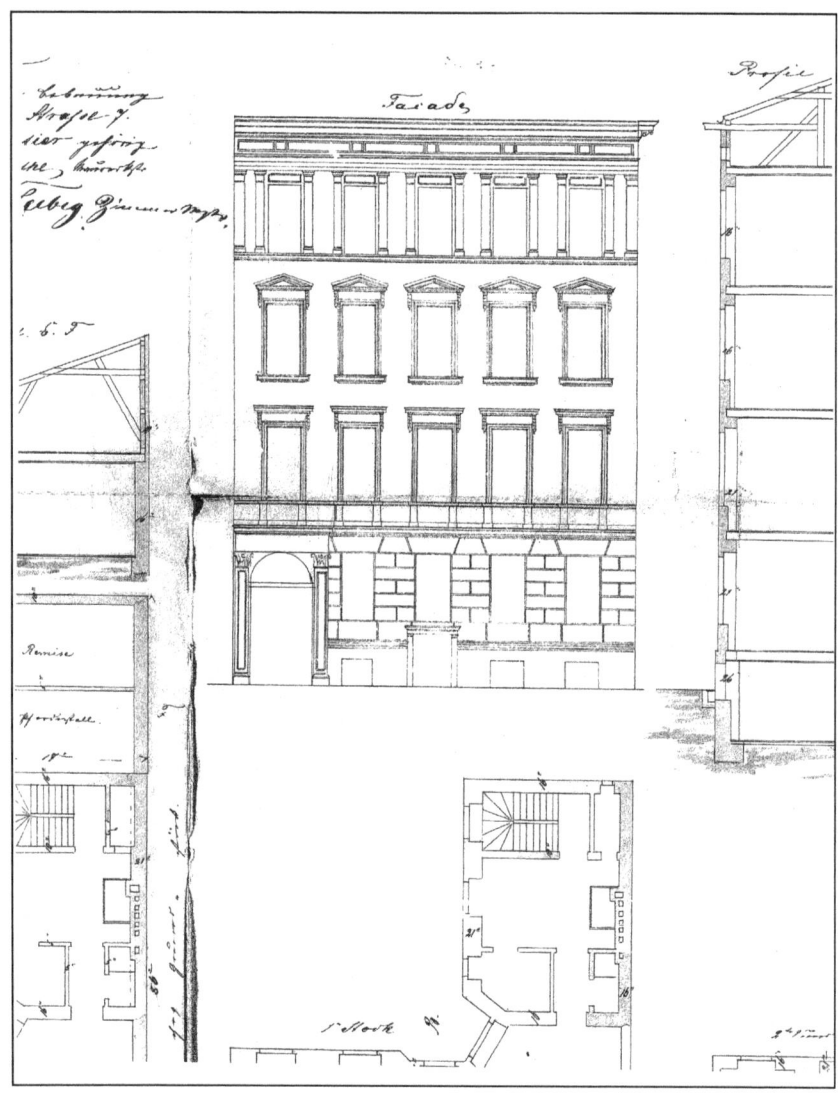

The façade as drawn in the 1865 application by the building police.

of the façade are available, so at least we have a good idea of what the Clemenses' house looked like. It was a five-story, twenty-four-year-old tenement, so it was not exactly built "last week," as Twain had claimed in his travel letter to Chicago, but it was still relatively new. It probably looked much like the houses at the adjacent Pohlstrasse, built at the same time, which still exist today. The courtyard

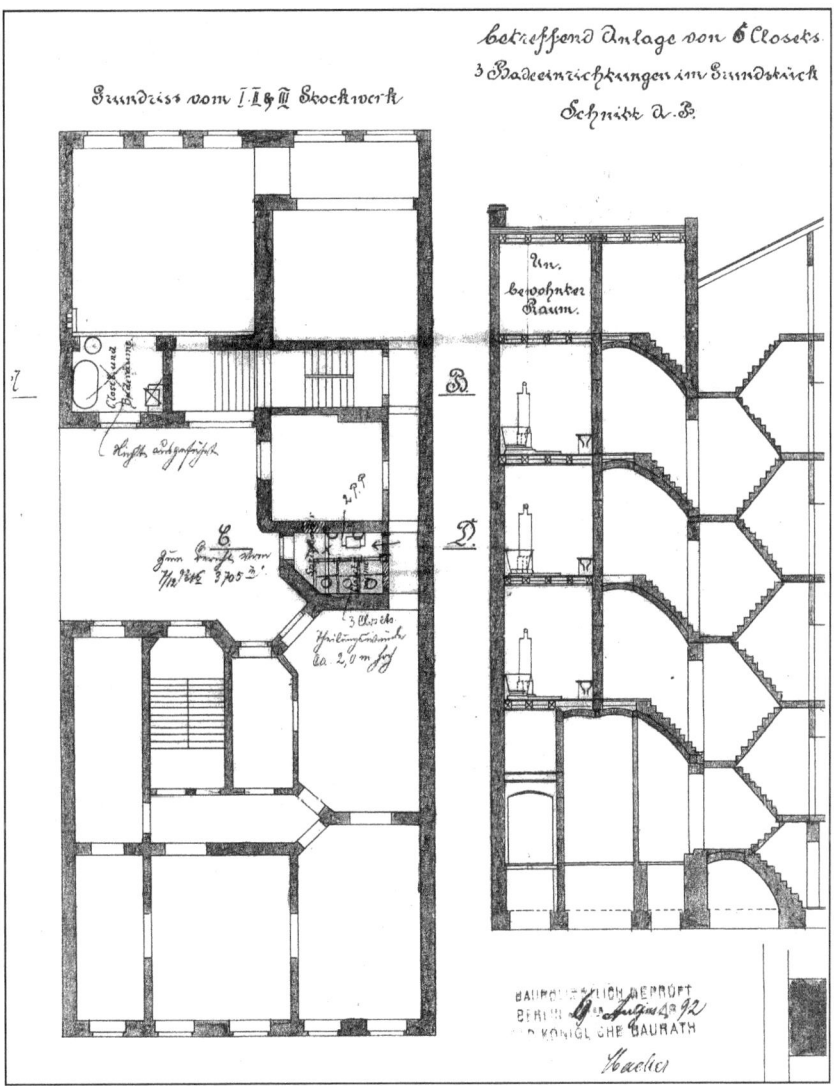

The floorplan of 7 Körnerstrasse, where the Clemenses lived in 1891.

of 7 Körnerstrasse encompassed a chicken coop and a pigeon loft, both made of stone. The family had a five-bedroom apartment on the second floor, with a bathroom, bathtub, and modern plumbing connected to the sewer system, but no electricity yet. Every night at ten o'clock, the porter extinguished the gas lamps in the stairwell. The apartment was also equipped with furniture "right down to the last pot in the kitchen and napkin in the cupboard," as the Berlin paper *National-Zeitung* would report somewhat later. Olivia also had to insist on getting table silver delivered, and they were charged extra for it. Twain complained a lot about the quality of the mattresses, which he considered to be too firm. He made the landlord bring new ones more than once, but that was only a change from "limestone to granite and from granite to conglomerate," as he claimed. Since he did a lot of writing sitting in his bed, a comfortable mattress was important to him.

Twain set himself up to work at Körnerstrasse right away, and he kept in constant touch with his New York publishing house, Charles Webster & Co., mostly by mail and telegram. Charles Webster was the husband of Twain's niece, and the author had tapped him to run his publishing business. But Twain was not satisfied with him, and, in addition, Webster had fallen ill at age thirty-seven. So Twain had turned over control to Webster's young assistant, Frederick Hall, in 1888, who did his best to comply with Twain's many demands. While in Berlin, Twain "put in a good deal of time devising publishing schemes, principal among them being a plan for various cheap editions of his books, pamphlets, and such like, to sell for a few cents," according to his biographer Albert Bigelow Paine. "These projects appear never to have been really undertaken, Hall very likely fearing that a flood of cheap issues would interfere with the more important trade."

Unfortunately, his poor health kept the author from doing as much writing as he would have liked. On October 16, Twain wrote his first letter to Hall; he complained that this was "the first time I have taken hold of a pen lately, but I will write a line or two, against the doctor's prohibition." He was thinking about a "boy story" he could offer to the McClure Syndicate. "But nothing seems to occur to me." He also told Hall that he was the only Clemens in the house on Körnerstrasse "and possibly in this town," so it should be easy for the postal service to find him (this is actually not true—Berlin had forty-eight Clemens' at that time). He ended the letter with, "I must stop—my arm is howling."

On the same day, he wrote a letter to Franklin G. Whitmore,

asking him to go to Paige and "remember me to him"—Whitmore was supervising the construction of the Paige typesetter on Twain's behalf. Four days later, Twain urged Hall to come up with a publishing schedule for his just-finished satirical novel, *The American Claimant,* which takes place in England and was the "first novel to not mention the weather," according to Twain. He had dictated most of the manuscript to a new phonographic device, a very early predecessor of the turntable. This was not yet commonly used, but he tried it because of his rheumatism.

In his diary, also in October, he noted some complaints about everyday life in Berlin. "So many little conveniences not to be had here: Fountain pens, good type-writing machines, rubber shoes." He asked his British publisher, Chatto & Windus, to send him a new Wirt fountain pen, "medium, neither too stiff nor too limber," since he had lost his and was "helpless" without one. He also asked for a copy of *The Table,* a cookbook his company, Webster & Co., had issued in New York.

Twain was much more successful immersing himself in Berlin's social life, and he became the center of the American expats' social circles. In those years, quite a few American diplomats, writers, artists, and businessmen lived in the German capital. James Dickie, pastor of the American Church in Berlin from 1894 to 1908, estimated in his book, *In the Kaiser's Capital,* that the expat community had about two thousand members, based on who was registered with the police. One of Twain's earliest friends was the American Ambassador William Walter Phelps, who originated from Philadelphia and New Jersey. He was nicknamed "Yaas" by Twain's daughters, because of his strange way of saying "yes." Phelps, who was a member of Congress and a Republican, was sent to Berlin in 1889, by President Benjamin Harrison. Twain had already known Phelps in America. One of Twain's first Berlin letters to the ambassador, presumably from October or November 1891, confirms an appointment for the following Sunday. "Church first—we shall be there promptly at 11 & as gay as the gayest—thence to breakfast, where we shall behave in a way to surprise & gratify you. Jean is too young to come (11

William Walter Phelps, the American Ambassador in 1891, and his attaché Theodore Bingham, who later became the New York police chief.

years), so we are obliged to decline for her." Twain had substituted "&" for "and," supposedly to save time. He did that often, and it was something his daughters loved to make fun of.

Twain met Phelps not only in his private residence—the ambassador lived at 57 Dorotheenstrasse, near Unter den Linden—but also at diplomatic events at the American embassy. The embassy was located at 66 Mohrenstrasse at first, in an office suite rented from a banking house, the *Kur- und Neumärkische Haupt-Ritterschaftliche Creditinstitut,* then one of many in the area. Sometime around 1891, however, the Ritterschaft management decided to build a bigger, more splendid edifice on its lot, so the embassy moved across the street into the Hotel Kaiserhof, at 1-5 Mohrenstrasse. The Hotel Kaiserhof was the first luxury hotel in Berlin, with electricity and a telephone in every room; Bismarck had used it once to

In 1891, the American embassy rented offices within this building at 66 Mohrenstrasse, then a bank. The statues depict Prussian generals.

invite European heads of state to an international conference. It is not known which one of the two locations Twain frequented, but it was most likely the latter. The Kaiserhof was destroyed in World War II. Today, the embassy of North Korea occupies the lot, while 66 Mohrenstrasse is the seat of the German Ministry of Health.

Twain also visited the embassy to sit there and write. For American correspondents, frequenting and utilizing diplomatic facilities was not all that uncommon. And Phelps, who was homesick, welcomed American visitors. Twain also got acquainted with the ambassador's attaché, Captain Theodore Bingham (who would later become an infamously ruthless police commissioner in New York City). Phelps's daughter Marian also became a dear friend of Twain. It was Marian's "youth, beauty, and cleverness (which) delighted Mark Twain in his troubled Berlin days," wrote Henry William Fisher in his book,

Hotel Kaiserhof, *the most luxurius hotel in Wilhelminian Berlin. The American Embassy was located here for a few months.*

Abroad with Mark Twain and Eugene Fields. Fisher was a fellow correspondent working for American papers such as *Harper's Weekly,* the *New York Sun,* and Joseph Pulitzer's *New York World;* he had met Twain in Chicago a few years earlier. However, while Fisher's writing is often amusing, he is not considered especially reliable by Mark Twain scholars (or anybody else, for that matter). His memories should be taken with a grain of salt. Marian Phelps later married Franz Johannes von Rottenburg, a high-ranking bureaucrat of the Foreign Service and a confidante of Bismarck; Twain called him Fritz. While the marriage didn't last, their son Phelps Phelps would become the first U.S. Governor of Samoa.

Fisher was not the only foreign correspondent Twain became acquainted with. He also met Henry du Pré Labouchère, a politician, publisher, and investigative journalist of the satirical British weekly *Truth*. Labouchère had become famous with his dispatches from the beleaguered city of Paris in the French-German war of 1870–71

The Kaiserhof has been replaced by the embassy of North Korea. On the left side, in the background, the flag of North Korea is flying.

he sent to the *Daily News* in London, a paper he co-owned. He was a British nobleman (in those days, foreign correspondents usually had a fancy backrgound) and Twain called him the "baron-maker," since he promoted supposedly droves of ordinary English folks to baronets and baronesses.

Twain also got to know Poultney Bigelow, an author and journalist for numerous American papers, who was born into a diplomatic American family, and grew up in Potsdam. Bigelow was friends with Prince Wilhelm—who would become Kaiser Wilhelm II—and the emperor's younger brother Henry (in addition to the Berlin city castle, the imperial house of Hohenzollern resided in numerous castles in Potsdam). A few months later, Twain asked Frederick Hall to send him an essay Bigelow had written about the Kaiser and German war policies.

Twain's visit took place during exciting times. Chancellor Otto von Bismarck, a count and a staunch conservative, who had been in charge first of Prussia, then of Germany for nearly thirty years, had just been dismissed by Kaiser Wilhelm II, who had inherited the throne in 1888. Bismarck is still remembered in Germany today as the man who unified the country, but also for his landmark legislation introducing social security and health care in the 1880s. Berlin has a number of streets, places, statues, and even a subway station honoring him.

Wilhelm II, however, had decided to put Leo von Caprivi in charge, a Prussian general, who was a little more prone to taking orders from him than the "iron" Bismarck. In his younger years, the Kaiser was by no means a Liberal by today's standards (outside of Texas), but he was a little less conservative than Bismarck. The Kaiser was militaristic and fond of weaponry and uniforms, and he also had a reputation for being vain and not that smart. Yet under his rule, Jews—at least the wealthier ones who would back him—and the substantial Polish minority in the eastern provinces, such as Silesia, were integrated. Also, laws for the protection of laborers and a progressive income tax were passed in the Reichstag by the German Parliament. During Twain's stay, the legislative body was located at 4 Leipziger Strasse, while today's famous Reichstag building was still under construction.

However, the undemocratic voting laws remained unchanged: men who paid more taxes had more votes. Twain would soon complain about the German tax laws, since they also affected him. When Twain arrived, these political battles were in full swing. After Bismarck resigned, he continued to be a force in politics, mostly by using the press, and several high-ranking bureaucrats remained secretly loyal to the Iron Chancellor. The American author never voiced an opinion in public. But there is reason to assume that he tended to prefer the Kaiser over Bismarck, whom he once called a "rascal," at least according to Fisher.

After Twain met the Kaiser in February 1892, he wrote in his diary that he was a "good man, better than his impulses, who wanted a change, wanted to see how my kind would go, was tired of high society." And about four years later in London, Twain made a compassionate note about Georg von Bunsen, a Liberal member of the

The Bismarck memorial in the Tiergarten, near the Victory Column. The "Iron Chancellor" ruled Prussia and Germany for over thirty years.

Kaiser Wilhelm II, the last Emperor of Germany, in his uniform. When the Emperor was young, Mark Twain was quite fond of him.

Prussian parliament and the Reichstag, who was dying at the time. Mrs. Poultney Bigelow had told him that Bunsen had "made a liberal speech which infuriated Bismarck," Twain wrote, and not only did Bismarck ignore Bunsen ostentatiously in public afterward; he intimidated his officers and generals from socializing with the Bunsen family, so five of their six daughters could not find husbands. One of them, Berta, eventually married Ernest Flagg Henderson, an American living in Berlin, who became a friend of the Clemenses.

Twain most likely never met the former Chancellor himself, since the retiree had left Berlin for the rural community of Friedrichsruh (even though he continued to meddle in German politics, mostly by using the press). Twain was, however, pleased to hear from Fisher that Bismarck liked his books, which he had gotten for Christmas. He even inquired how Fisher knew that Bismarck had actually read them, whereupon Fisher said, "Because he asked me whether there are still steamer loads of Yankees going picnicking in Palestine with Mark Twain for a bear-leader." He was referring to a scene from *The Innocents Abroad*.

Twain also had relatives in Berlin: a distant cousin, Alice von Versen, née Clemens. She was the daughter of Senator James Clemens Jr. and his wife Eliza, from St. Louis, Missouri, one of the couple's twelve children. The Senator, a descendant of immigrants from Leicestershire, England, was Twain's great-granduncle and always helpful to Twain's impoverished family. Alice was married to Lieutenant General Maximilian von Versen, who had been promoted to adjutant general to the Kaiser. This made the couple part of the emperor's court. According to Mally Wenske, a contemporary family relative in Germany, the couple met while Alice was visiting Berlin with her father. They got engaged in Dresden in 1870, but they kept their relationship secret at first, because Maximilian was about to be sent to the war between Germany and France. General von Versen knew America well from his many travels. He had even met the brother of his future wife in St. Louis in 1869, and they had become friends. While active in the Prussian Army, he fought in the war between Paraguay and Brazil, and made a request to join the American Civil War as well—though it is not known on which

Alice Clemens and Maximilian von Versen resided at 36 Mauerstrasse.

side. Prussia was officially neutral, though in fact it sided with the North (while England endorsed the South), so von Versen most likely wanted to join the Union. His request, however, was turned down. The couple had five children; the oldest, a daughter named Hulda, was Susy's age, while the youngest, Elizabeth Alice, was two when Twain met them. The family resided close to the Brandenburg Gate, in a townhouse at 36 Mauerstrasse (an address where the famed poet Rahel Varnhagen had lived in the 1820s).

Twain was no fan of the military, but he was impressed by von Versen's tenacity. He read the general's notes about his adventures in the war between Paraguay, Brazil, Argentina, and Uruguay, and commented in his diary, "Have seen many high military officers—majors general, etc., [but this is] a General—a whole General—without any qualifying word in front of the title—that is a rare sight to me—& if I had been Gen v. V. I should have *grown* somewhat

The house at 36 Mauerstrasse is gone. A playground occupies the lot.

in the last 2 mos., but I don't see that his size has been affected." (von Versen was not very tall). He also called the general "genuinely modest," whose "account of his perilous running the gauntlet 25 yrs ago between the Brazilian & Paraguayan lines reads as modestly and unconsciously as a Sunday School Pleasure excursion." As a writer, however, Twain found him not especially effective. "He got about a page of literature out of that daring performance—just the mere bald unadorned *facts*. If I had done that thing, I shd. got 3 or 4 books out of it—& not a fact in them anywhere."

Twain became a frequent guest not only at the von Versen dinner parties, but was invited to other diplomatic and social events as well. One of the first celebrations Twain attended was on October 13, 1891, at the Royal University—Friedrich Wilhelm University, called Humboldt University today—located on Unter den Linden. It was the 70th birthday of two prominent scientists, Rudolf Virchow

Left: General von Versen, the husband of Twain's cousin Alice Clemens. Right: Rudolf Virchow, the physician who challenged Bismarck.

and Hermann von Helmholtz (who were born within weeks of each other). Virchow was a pathologist who did groundbreaking research on typhus and leukemia. He is regarded as the father of social medicine—the theory that diseases have their roots in living conditions—and he was a Progressive Party member of the Reichstag. Virchow became a staunch opponent of Bismarck, who challenged him to a duel after the scientist had criticized his exuberant military spending. Due to tradition, it was up to Virchow to choose the weapons. He suggested they slap each other with pork sausages infected with salmonella. Bismarck declined. Helmholtz was a physicist, whose research in the field of energy led to the development of motor engines.

The festivities culminated in a "commers," a social gathering of fraternity students. The "commers" took place in a huge hall, "beautifully decorated with clustered flags and various ornamental devices," as Twain wrote in his travel letter to Chicago, with up to four thousand guests, among them thousand students, attend-

Left: Hermann von Helmholtz, whose inventions led to the motor car.
Right: Theodor Mommsen, the historian who resembled Mark Twain (a bit).

ing. "All these intent and worshiping eyes were centered upon one spot—the place where Virchow and Helmholtz sat." Then a "concealed band played a piece of martial music; followed by a pause. The students on the platform rose to their feet, the middle one gave a toast to the Emperor, then all the house rose, mugs in hand." After lots and lots of beer, a late guest was about to arrive. Twain saw at the far end of the hall a "silken gleam and the lifted swords of a guard of honor plowing through the remote crowds." Then, the students on the platform rose to their feet, "like a wave. This supreme honor had been offered to no one before. Then there was an excited whisper at our table—'Mommsen!'—and the whole house rose. Rose and shouted and stamped and clapped, and banged the beer-mugs. Then the little man with his long hair and Emersonian face edged his way past us and took his seat. I could have touched him with my hand—Mommsen!—think of it!"

Theodor Mommsen was the most renowned historian of the 19th

century; in 1902, he received the Nobel Prize for his work on Roman history (his grandson, Theodor Ernst Mommsen, immigrated to the United States in 1936, and became a professor at Cornell). Twain was thrilled—"I would have walked a great many miles to get a sight of him." He also got a kick out of their visual similarity. "Been mistaken for Mommsen twice," he wrote in his diary. "We have the same hair, but on examination, it was found the brains were different." Mix-ups like this had happened to him before. His daughter Clara revealed to *The New York Times* that Twain had been mistaken for Buffalo Bill in London. However, when Twain walked home from the celebration (together with Henry Fisher), he became sentimental. "Virchow is seventy years old," he said. "In a little while he will either be dead or that great intellect of his will begin to deteriorate, and what a pity that would be!"

Twain had a good time in Berlin, but he soon grew weary of Körnerstrasse. In his diary, Twain referred to Körnerstrasse as a "rag-pickers' paradise," and as "slum-land." And his American friends thought likewise, as his biographer Bigelow Paine pointed out. "Semi-acquaintances said, 'Ah, yes, Körnerstrasse,' acquaintances said, 'Dear me, do you like it?' An old friend exclaimed, 'Good gracious! How in the world did you ever come to locate there?'" Twain blamed the real estate agent who had promised him an upscale address near Potsdamer Platz, where nobility, such as dukes, lived in droves. "They shall be as common to your eye as the daisies in the fields." The realtor was one Mr. Prächtel, whom Twain called "Mr. P." When the author pointed out to Mr. P. that, upon looking at the windows of Körnerstrasse, he "never saw so many women of any profession gazing at nothing before—and absorbed in it," the realtor assured him that those women were really "duchesses, who sleep all day in that manner," tired out because they "dance all night at the court halls."

For Twain's daughters, too, Körnerstrasse was a descent from the social and economic status to which they were accustomed, and they made sure to let it be known. In her memoirs, Clara recalled "noisy children who played in the muddy streets," and "un-kempt, half-clad women [who] were continually leaning out the windows opposite us, their elbows propped on comfortable cushions." With sarcasm inherited from her father, she added that "they feared missing a street fight or two." She also mentioned a "rag warehouse" on the street. And Jean wrote in her diary, "We all of us hated the street." She also disclosed that "the first cook we had was a thief and stole the same night that she was dismissed."

The family complained not only about the lack of noblemen, they were even more bothered by the noise. Körnerstrasse, east of Potsdamer Strasse, was close to a noisy railway junction and to the tracks of the Potsdamer and Anhalter train stations. Twain believed that the street must be "unquestionably the noisiest one in the whole earth." The entire family lost its "cheerfulness," he noted in his diary, because of the noise. Unfortunately, they had picked a place on the "wrong side" of this Tiergarten neighborhood. The "better side" was located west of Potsdamer Strasse—the *Kielganviertel*, an upscale area lined with beautiful mansions. We still get an idea of what the *Kielganviertel* was like by visiting the Café Einstein, the former mansion of silent film star Henny Porten. Today, the Einstein is a hangout for literary folks (and wannabes), whereas Körnerstrasse is still populated with noisy, now mostly Turkish children playing in the street.

According to Fisher, Twain had confirmed the rental contract only because two cats had been living in the apartment (supposedly, Olivia had brought them along). Twain had a big heart for cats, and he always had cats living with him—in Hartford, there were several felines. And it had been Olivia anyway who had made that decision. Twain's wife had already arrived in Berlin with her sister Susan in August 1891, to look for a rental. Her choice reflected her desire to save money, and she was by no means unhappy. She even wrote to her friend Harriet Whitmore that they had successfully secured a "pleasant, sunny apartment" for themselves. Her husband did not share that sentiment. But his—slightly exaggerated—account about the experience, *On Renting a Flat in Berlin,* didn't get published then, because Olivia forbade it. She found it embarrassing.

On Renting a Flat in Berlin

By Mark Twain

I came on toward the end of summer to prepare a house for the winter. I came posted—partially. What is to say, I had been told that in Berlin one engages a flat in an empty condition and hires furniture for it by the year. The first thing I did was to make a mistake. I ought to have gone to our Consul General or to our Minister and asked a lot of useful questions. But that would not have been American fashion and so I did not do it. The American fashion is, to know it all yourself, to bull along in your own hap-hazard way and ask nobody's help.

I stated my case to a person whom I did know, and he was very obliging. He told me to go Mr. P. in the Krausenstrasse and put myself into his hands—he would be a mother to me. I went to my new mother and found him all graciousness. He was a handsome man and not old, not even elderly; his manners were pleasant and easy and very, very smooth and he talked good English.

"Do you wish an expensive Wohnung?"

A Wohnung. The reader will understand, is a dwelling and in Berlin is the usual term for a "flat."

"I wish a quiet one—that is the main thing."

"Are you intending to go into society?"

"I? Oh, no; I don't know anybody in Berlin. The society I can see from the window will have to answer, I judge."

He thought a moment and said:

"How would you like to be located where you could look out on the best society in Berlin every day—the very loftiest society in this capital outside the imperial palace?"

His eye glowed and there was emotion in his voice. I caught the infection and said with strong feeling—

"You don't mean the nobility?"

He nodded his head several times with an assent too deep for words. We grasped hands in silence and shook and shook. When he got his voice, he said—

"You shall live in the very midst. They shall be as common to your eye as the daisies in the fields. Promise yourself this happiness, for it shall be yours."

The generous tears stood in his eyes and to mine all things were blurred with an ascending moisture. He called his assistant and sent us forth on our quest. We examined some very handsome apartments, attractively situated—some on the great and rich thoroughfare called the Potsdamerstrasse, others on the banks of the pretty canal with shade trees and darling glimpses of the wavy water and the bridges. But always there was an objection on the part of the assistant:

"This region is too commercial—smells of trade";

"This locality will not answer—no nobility here. The aristocracy shun this district."

These verdicts brought me a pang everytime, for those places were very enticing; and some of them seemed to me almost the most beautiful in this beautiful city. However, at last the assistant found a street and a house that satisfied even his pampered taste. He was greatly moved and said softly and lovingly—

"Ah Körnerstreet, Körnerstreet, why did I not think of you before! A place fit for the gods, dear sir. Quiet?—Notice how still it is and remember this is noonday—noonday. It is but one block long, you see—just a sweet dear little nest hid away here in the heart of the great metropolis, its presence and its sacred quiet unsuspected by the restless crowds that swarm along the stately thoroughfares yonder at its two extremities. And—"

"But it doesn't smell very good—do you think it does?"

"That smell? That is not from here—this street is not to blame for that—that comes from those other streets."

"Still I don't see ….. that the smell smells about the same way that it would smell if it were this street's own smell instead of a smell that is properly taxable in those other streets."

"No, you are wrong there, quite wrong. And besides—this building is handsome, but I don't think much of the others. They look pretty commonplace compared to the rest of Berlin."

"Dear-dear! Have you noticed that? It is just an affectation of the nobility. What they want…"

"The nobility? Do they live in…"

"…in this street? That is good!—very good indeed. I wish the Duke of Sassafras-Hagenstein could hear you say that. When the Duke first moved in here, he…"

"Does he live in this street?"

"Him! Well I should say so! Do you see the big plain house over there with the placard in the third-floor window? That's his house."

"The placard that says 'Furnished rooms to let?' Does he keep boarders?"

"What an idea! Him! With a rent-roll of twelve hundred thousand marks a year? Oh positively this is too good."

"Well what does he have that sign up for?"

The assistant took me by the buttonhole, and said with a merry light beaming in his eye—

"Why, my dear sir, a person would know you are new to Berlin just by your innocent questions. Our aristocracy—our old real genuine aristocracy—are full of the quaintest eccentricities, eccentricities inherited for centuries which they are prouder of than they are of their titles, and that sign-board there is one of them. They all hang that out. And it's regulated by an unwritten law. A baron is entitled to hang out two, a count five, a duke fifteen—"

"Then they are all dukes over on that side I sup—"

"Every one of them. Now the old duke of Backofenhofen-Schwartz—not the present duke, but the last one, he—"

"Does he live over the sausage shop there in the cellar?"

"No, the one further along, where the eighteenth yellow cat is chewing the door-mat where the equerry split the liver and tripe when he stumbled a minute ago. There—over there—don't you see?"

"But all the yellow cats are chewing the door mats."

Yes, but I mean the eighteenth one. Count. No, never mind; there's a lot more come. I'll get you another mark. Let me see—"

"Do you mean the house where all those brisk particulars are on the sign-board—where they sell cow's milk and rago and keep a junk-shop in the cellar?"

"The next one to that, the next one to that!—to the right."

"Yes, I see now—the one with the sand-pile in front and the sick dog hitched to the coal cart."

"That's the one, it's the very one."

"Is that the duke's dog?"

"Yes—he's a hunting dog."

"Hunting dog?—that animal?"

"Yes–elephant dog. Very fine dog—very fine breed."

"What do they hitch him in the coal cart for?"

"To keep him in practice—keep him strong."

"It doesn't work I reckon; he is not fat, and he looks pretty serious."

"Yes, he hasn't had enough practice yet, but he'll pull up as he gets his hand in."

"What does the duke want with elephant dogs in Germany?"

"Just for style, merely for style; they all keep them—the nobility, I mean."

"Ratters would come good in this alley, don't you think?"

"Alley! This is no alley. It is an esplanade; that is what it is. And it's the only one in Berlin that is named after a poet."

"What harm had he done?"

"Him? He didn't do any harm at all; and he wrote some of the noblest poems in his language. He died early. He died just as they were going to name this esplanade for him."

"Heard of it, I reckon."

"I think one reason was—"

"There's eleven chambermaids lolling out of the window over there; they are lolling all along the row; I never saw so many idle chambermaids before; and I never saw so many women of any profession gazing at nothing before—and absorbed in it."

"Chambermaids—listen to that! They are duchesses, that is what they are. They hang out of those windows all day. Often they go to sleep hanging out that way. Some of those are asleep now—most of them are. They dance all night at the court halls and then air—off all day like that and sleep. The most romantic people—they would die if they couldn't be romantic. They lead a charmed life, those dutchesses."

"But some of them are alive; now what are they looking at? There's nothing to see but the wagon that's being loaded with bones and bottles and ashes and the sick elephant dog and the vast bales of rags that those two pale peasant women are hauling up out of that cellar with cottonhooks. I never saw women doing work like that before; but they do it well, sad and tired as they look, poor creatures. Tell me—do you see several children over there rooting in the sand pile?"

"Yes—forty-three. I've counted them. Do they all live in the block?"

"Yes and there's others. It's an elegant place for children—healthy, salubrious, fertile. It's the most fertile street there is."

"Are they noble?"

"The bluest blood in the kingdom. All of them—everyone."

"I begin to like this esplanade very much. One thing I like about it is the paucity of the dogs."

The Assistant was silent—so silent that I was afraid he was dead. Later I was sorry he wasn't.

Upon inspection the Wohnung proved to be commodious, clean and comfortable and at the rear it had a pleasant outlook upon a large garden. We went back to headquarters and I engaged it for six months at what seemed a very reasonable price considering the guest privileges I was going to have. We drew up a boiler-iron contract for the mutual protection of Mr. P. and his furniture and then I arranged about the advance payments and took the rail for Bohemia again, pleased with myself for having carried this business through in good shape without the help of the American minister or anybody else.

A month later we all arrived in Berlin and went to housekeeping. The furniture was pretty poor and pretty cheap and comically pretentious and all that but I thought it was Berlin style and I was quite satisfied and happy. True, I did not warm to the ancient curtains of the "salon" much, because as a rule I do not care for antiquities but I made no moan. As the beds—I didn't really like the beds—that is the austere solidity of them. They were well enough, perhaps, but they kept reminding me of geological strata to sleep on. Mr. P. changed the mattresses several times but without noticeable result; it was merely a change from limestone to granite and from granite to conglomerate and did no real good. I showed him a place where he could get mattresses fit for the sheet to sleep on, but he explained that he did not own those and therefore was not able to command them. He furnished silver, but charged extra for it, that detail having been overlooked in the contract. Also there was a stove in one of the rooms that turned cold and froze the rest of the furniture solid every time we built a fire in it.

However, all these were matters of small moment and we sailed along pleasantly enough. I waited with a kind of eager expectancy for a chance to spring the style of our neighbors on the family and see them stare and exult. Finally I had my opportunity and it made me feel good. They asked—

"Who are the people over the way?"

"Dukes, every one!"

"Dukes? Do Dukes look like that?"

"In Berlin the do; it's their way; the most eccentric people in the world."

"Who said they were Dukes?"

"Mr. P.'s Assistant."

"It must be true, then, no doubt, but they are a great disappointment."

The days drifted along and I've began to get reacquainted with people. Whenever I was asked where we lived I tried to bring out the name of the street with modesty, but my pride in it was …… apparent—I couldn't help it. Then it hurt me to see that they never applauded, they never even looked enviously surprised. Finally somebody said—

"Isn't it pretty noisy?"

"Noisy? Körnerstrasse?"

"Yes—nights."

That was true. I had been trying to disguise it from myself. From this moment I was not able to do that any longer. Yes it was noisy. It was not merely noisy in a general citified way, it was noisy in a way of its own. That is to say, the night was made up of deep stretches of silence broken to smash at irregular intervals by the thundering rush of heavy wagons that made the house quake and brought us broad awake and quivering. A half hour's sleep, then another awful rush and roar over the rough stone pavement. Another interval, then a half a dozen people would tramp through the short street whooping and howling and laughing and screeching like maniacs. Toward morning—every morning—somebody came through, stopping before each house and clanging a sharp-tongued bell—The milkman perhaps. Then the dogs!—but we will not talk about that. Yes it was a noisy street—unquestionably the noisiest one in the whole earth. We wasted away under the torture of broken sleep and began to lose our cheerfulness.

By the by we began to encounter frank people who stared in a bewildered way for a while after hearing that we lived in Körnerstrasse and then caught their breath and gasped out just the brief remark—

"Du lieber Gott!"

Being pressed for an explanation, they would say—

"But you *don't* mean to say you *live* in that street? Who put you innocents there?"

"Mr. P. of Krausenstrasse."

"Ah—that accounts for it."

Several—in fact, couple of hundred—asked:

"What do you pay him?"

And when I told them, they said—

"Three full and complete prices! Well you have been superbly gouged."

That is true enough, but there is nothing remarkable about it. Mr. P. is not any worse than some of his brethren in the same trade here. His furniture is worse, perhaps, but he himself isn't. Besides, it is quite easy to protect oneself from these people. Instead of going to the man's pal, as I did, the stranger should go to his country's legislation and ask about prices for flats and furniture and then go about his affair in a rational way. I am not the first foreigner who has furnished profit and amusement to professional house-furnishers of Berlin. So there is a long procession of these mourners every year. A long procession; and yet to speak the truth, I did fare a little worse than any of the others, for I am the only one that struck bottom—that is to say Körnerstrasse; and as for dukes—why the place was absolutely barren of them.

Evidently, Twain did not get the promised "noble neighbors"—according to the 1892 Berlin address book, not one single duke or duchess resided on Körnerstrasse. But that didn't mean that only poor people and "dirty noisy children" lived there. The street was occupied by a number of factory workers, but also by a fish merchant, two train engineers, and a few widows—quite possibly the ones watching the street from their windows all day, as Clara described it. Some high-ranking Prussian officials also lived on Körnerstrasse, including a ministerial director, and a few army officers, such as two cavalry captains, an army colonel, and a lieutenant colonel—and even a banker. The owner of the house, Mr. Killisch, was a *Rittmeister a. D.* as well, which translates as "retired cavalry captain."

So, Körnerstrasse was not such a "slum land" after all, but a rather mixed neighborhood. Not only did Theodor Fontane and the aforementioned painter Anton von Werner reside close by, also the author Hermann Sudermann lived right around the corner, on Lützowstrasse. Though his name is not well known today, Sudermann's play, *Die Ehre* ("Honor") was a huge success in 1891, and he became one of the best-paid German authors. However, Sudermann purchased a castle outside of Berlin right away with his abundant earnings, so Twain never met him.

The Berlin address book also indicates a lumberyard three houses down, which had been there for thirty years. This was most likely Clara's "rag warehouse." The lumberyard was probably the last remainder of the street's agricultural past. Until 1860, the whole area had been farmland, and the only buildings in the area lined the main thoroughfare, Potsdamer Strasse, while Körnerstrasse did not even exist. That changed in 1862, when City Hall adopted the so-called Hobrecht Plan, a land-use plan named after James Hobrecht, who was an engineer and worked for the royal Prussian planning police, the institution in charge of urban planning. The Hobrecht Plan mapped the new urban grid within the newly expanded city limits, since the sprawling city urgently needed housing for the masses of immigrant workers. The Hobrecht Plan was also the main reason for the Clemenses' unhappiness. According to the plan, real estate owners were obliged to pay taxes according to the width of the street-facing front of the tenements, not the size of the lot itself. And so the classic Berlin tenement came into existence; magnificent, yet narrow fronted houses with many compactly built rear buildings accessible through doorways and backyards.

The upper classes—army officers, doctors, university professors, bank directors—lived in the front part of the tenements, facing the street, preferably in the cherished Bel Etage, the second floor. The first building in the backyards housed the less prosperous classes—City Hall clerks, elementary school teachers, grocers. And poor factory workers, many of them immigrants, lived in the second or maybe even the third backyards, in much more cramped quarters, with less sunlight, and often with only one shared bathroom for the whole floor. In this manner, Berlin housed people from a variety of socio-economic backgrounds together in the same block. This was an unusual arrangement for Americans used to neighborhoods designated and separated by both race and class.

Twenty years later, Bigelow Paine visited Körnerstrasse. He found the street to be cleaner than Twain had described it in the 1890s. "It is still not aristocratic, but it is eminently respectable," he wrote. The house at 7, however, had been replaced by a neo-gothic, red brick structure resembling a knight's castle. The German *Reichspost*, the Imperial Postal Office, had commissioned the building for a telecommunications facility for telegrams and wires. Three tenements were taken down to make way for the postal building, including the one in which the Clemens family had lived. Paine talked to some of the postal clerks during his visit, who all knew the name Mark Twain and his books, since they were translated into German early on. However, no one was aware that the author had actually lived at that very place. Today, a plaque on the façade of the telecommunications building (which survived World War II), hung by the Berlin city government, informs passers-by of the famous visitor of the Gilded Age.

Above: Körnerstrasse No 7 was torn down for the Telecommunications Agency. It is still there. A plaque memorializing Twain adorns the door.

Twain would soon find out what it meant to live in a Prussian city: He clashed constantly with the abundant bureaucracy and the police. "Berlin seems to be the most governed city in the world, but one must admit that it also seems to be the best governed," he wrote in his travel letter to Chicago. "The Berlin government has a rule for everything, and puts the rule in force...with great matters and minute particulars with equal faithfulness, and with a plodding and painstaking diligence and persistence which compel admiration—and sometimes regret." He recognized early on that most Americans felt differently about authority from not only Prussians, but Europeans in general. "Europe has lived a life of hypocrisy for ages," he wrote in his diary, "it is so ingrained in flesh & blood that sincere speech is impossible to these people when speaking of hereditary power. 'God Save the King' is uttered millions of times a day in Europe . . . Even Luther strongly reprobated rebellion against constituted (no matter how) authority. The first gospel of all monarchies should be Rebellion . . . against Church & State."

One issue Twain fretted about was that he had to register with the Prussian police within six days of arrival, like every visitor. Naturally, the police registered him under his real name "Clemens, S. L.," the initials standing for "Samuel Langhorne." The Berlin address book of 1892 indicates him as "'Privatier' (i.e. man of independent means), W. Körnerstraße 7, 1." "W" stands for West, today the borough of Tiergarten, and "1" indicates the first floor. That would be the second floor, by American reckoning. But that would not be the end of it. The 1891 edition of the *Baedeker* guidebook, *Berlin and its Surroundings,* pointed out that those who wanted to rent an apartment had to fill out a three-part mandatory questionnaire, and so had the author. In addition, the police kept prodding him for six weeks to get a passport for one of his maids, who was Swiss. Katie Leary, the American maid Twain had brought from Hartford, had left for the United States soon after, but he had hired three new maids in Germany.

Twain could have used the advice of James Dickie, who was well acquainted with Prussian etiquette, but alas, Twain only met Dickie

The old American Church at Motzstrasse, near Nollendorfplatz was built shortly after Twain left Berlin. It was destroyed in World War II.

upon the pastor's return to New York City. In his book, *In the Kaiser's Capital,* the pastor recommended not making one single mistake when handing over said questionnaire to the authorities. Dickie especially warned American ladies who might try to make themselves younger on paper. But he also knew of one lady who documented herself as five years older, for unknown reasons. "She went home to America for a few years and when she came back, it was incumbent on her to record her age as before; otherwise she would have had many disagreeable hours with the police."

In addition, whatever the officials documented, they never, ever forgot. Pastor Dickie mentioned another American, who, annoyed by the many questions he was asked, wrote "Mohammedan" [i. e. Muslim] for his "Religious Affiliation." When he wrote "Evangelical Protestant" on his following visit to Berlin a few years later, he

The new American Church is still located in Schöneberg, at Dennewitzplatz near the elevated train. It offers Sunday services in English.

found himself in a long and intense interrogation session that only ended when he claimed he had converted between visits.

Twain started to write during his first weeks on Körnerstrasse. "I have worked myself to death the last 3 days & nights translating (& making a neat copy of the translation) the most celebrated child's book in Europe, & today I mail it to you," he wrote to Frederick Hall on October 27. "It should be in your hands Nov. 7, I judge. I want it on the American market Dec. 10 to catch the holidays." The book he was so jubilantly talking about was *Struwwelpeter*, titled *Slovenly Peter* by Twain. The book tells children, in a somewhat gruesome manner, how to behave. But Twain was not attracted by the moral lessons, as his daughter Clara would write in the preface years later. It was much rather the "impious spirit of contrariness in the verses that appealed to Father, suffering as he was from the

Blue Berlin mood of those first weeks. He could sympathize with Kaspar, who wouldn't take his soup, because Father did not care for German soup either."

Twain was very excited about the project. He advised Hall to use "very large & clear type," and "bright lively color." The book was usually reprinted in black and white, and Twain wanted to improve upon that. However, in his enthusiasm, he had neglected to secure the copyright from the German author, Heinrich Hoffmann. The project failed to materialize. The U.S. edition did not appear until 1935, long after Twain's death, and only because Clara kept pursuing it. Twain also wanted to translate Hans Christian Andersen's sad story about the *Little Match Girl,* who dies in the snow, but he never succeeded in that either. Later, in mid-November, he suggested a book based on his travel letters from Europe, *Recent European Glimpses*. He was not really satisfied with the title, though. "I approve your several suggestions," he wrote to Hall, signing off, "Lamely yrs, SLC."

On Körnerstrasse, he also finished the first two of his six travel letters for McClure. The first one described the French city Aix-Les-Bain; the second one was about Bayreuth, titled, "At the Shrine of St. Wagner." The *Chicago Daily Tribune* and the *New York Sun* published them both on November 8 and December 6, 1891, respectively. Twain asked Hall to send him three copies, since he had promised to give one to his British colleague Henry Labouchère. A third letter, describing his travel from Aix to Bayreuth, followed soonafter.

Upon his arrival, Twain was by no means unknown in Berlin, and he soon became the toast of the town. "His popularity in Germany was openly manifested," wrote his biographer Bigelow Paine. "At any gathering he was surrounded by a brilliant company, eager to do him honor." This should be no surprise: his books had been translated into German for the last seventeen years, in almost thirty editions. And he happily noted that many of his books were on the display shelves in bookstores around the city. Twain's German publisher, Robert Lutz, who resided in Stuttgart, even used the opportunity of Twain's visit to distribute a six-volume edition of Twain's *Collected Works* in 1892. There was no other English-language author that was read as often as Mark Twain in those days in Germany. Robert M. Rodney, an American literature professor, points this out in his 1993 book, *Mark Twain Overseas*: "He traveled overseas more frequently and more extensively than any American celebrity of his time; and with the probable exception of Benjamin Franklin, he made a stronger and more lasting impact than any of his compatriots abroad."

Twain had a reputation as a respected journalist in Berlin as well, since some of his articles had been translated for German newspapers. During his visit, the *Berliner Börsenkurier*, a daily paper devoted to the coverage of the stock exchange, published a Twain piece titled, *Mental Telegraphy*, written in 1891 for *Harper's Monthly Magazine*. The story, which dealt with psychic abilities, made a big splash. Twain kept getting letters from American and German readers alike, who were interested in the topic, sent to his Berlin address. So it was no surprise that the Berlin press quickly jumped at the opportunity to interview Twain, beginning with Max Horwitz from the liberal-conservative *National-Zeitung*. Horwitz was a forty-eight-year-old German Jewish reporter who lived in Chicago for a couple of years; he had worked for the German-language paper *Illinois Staats-Zeitung*. Whether he knew Twain from this time is unknown, but according to Vic Fischer, a researcher with the Mark Twain Papers in Berkeley, Twain had numerous friends and acquaintances within the Chicago press.

On November 15, 1891, the *National-Zeitung* printed Horwitz's home story in its Sunday supplement. According to that story, the real Twain was quite different from what readers might expect, especially those who knew him only from his very own clichéd Wild West description of the offices of a fictional Kentucky paper. At this paper—Horwitz wrote—the editor dealt with his subscribers "only armed to the teeth, a revolver in his back pocket, a bowie knife in his belt." Horwitz seems to confuse this with a story Twain wrote about some fictional papers in Tennessee; the *Earthquake,* the *Higginsville Thunderbolt,* the *Battle Cry of Freedom,* and *The Daily Hurrah*. But for a German audience, Kentucky and Tennessee were probably one and the same anyway. But Twain wore "neither a gun nor a bowie knife in his belt," according to Horwitz's description.

The American was a "charming host, medium build, a somewhat weak body topped by a head framed by thick, bushy, and long, graying hair, whose moustache, though, still clearly shows its former dark blond color." When he met the reporter, Twain extended his left hand in greeting, because of the rheumatism in his painful, overworked right arm (he had also written to Chatto & Windus again, and requested an extra fountain pen, because the first one was too stiff for the ailing writer after all). Twain, according to Horwitz, complains "most of all about being forbidden to write his own entries in his notebook."

Horwitz asked whether Twain was planning a book about Berlin, something he would be "doubly interested" in. Twain assured him that the city was very enjoyable. "What beautiful architecture there is in the various streets, with alternating balconies and additions lined up one after another; yet far more impressive and agreeable is the city's light face, the bright colors, the friendly, welcoming tone of the facades." However, this made it difficult to write a satirical book, Twain explained, since he didn't want to set a bad example. "That is exactly what bothers us Americans so often—if I may be so bold—when you Europeans come over to us and enjoy our hospitality and protection under our laws, but then describe the trip with unmistakable arrogance, disparaging whatever springs into view and seems foreign, without even trying to get to the bottom of it." While the two were chitchatting for over an hour, dogs were barking outside. Twain, who hated dogs, was irritated. He interrupted the interview and told the reporter that he suspected there was an organized dogs' choir club on Körnerstrasse.

Later, Twain became quite friendly with Horwitz. He noted in his diary days after the interview that he would like Horwitz to "show him the ropes" (he uses a literal and somewhat flawed German translation, "die Seile mir lehren"), meaning, probably, to teach him German. Later, the Clemenses were invited by Horwitz and his wife to dine at their home.

Nine days after Horwitz's story ran, the liberal *Breslauer Morgen-Zeitung* published another piece about the "outstanding satirical American writer of our time." This (unnamed) reporter described

Twain as a "Yankee from head to toe, and unshakably apathetic. Even if his house were on fire, he would not get up from his desk or even dry his quill on the blotter and set it aside, annoyed, until the firemen flooded the room with water." However, "for the time being, Mark Twain cannot even pick up a quill; he suffers from rheumatism in his right arm."

The reporter was a little disappointed, though, that Twain did not bubble over with anecdotes and witty remarks. Instead, the American proved to be a characteristically slow talker and a difficult nut to crack. Twain, meanwhile, was astonished by the attempt to interview him. "Why? To publish something about it in the papers? But I can do a far better job of that myself!" He did eventually volunteer the information that his "favorite German poet is Heinrich Heine," and that he finds Berlin to be "terribly clean." The reporter leaves the author, hoping for a "delightful chapter by the great humorist about his adventures in a Berlin taxi-cab, hauled by an alleged horse."

Twain got around in Berlin by cabs and streetcars, both of which were horse-drawn then. Berlin had had horse-drawn busses and trolley cars since 1865; the first one ran between the Brandenburg Gate and Charlottenburg. When Twain came, there were numerous lines, including one on Potsdamer Strasse. The world's first electric streetcar was in the suburb of Lichterfelde, where it had already been running for about ten years. Twain described riding in them in great length in his essay, *The Chicago of Europe*. He was told by a native Berliner (so he claimed) that when the first streetcar had arrived, nearly thirty years prior, the public was so terrified of it that they didn't feel safe inside of it. So nobody would travel in the car "except convicts on the way to the gallows. This made business in only one direction, and the car had to go back light. To save the company, the city government transferred the convict cemetery to the other end of the line. This made traffic run in both directions and kept the company from going under." Twain added, "This sounds like some of the information which traveling foreigners are furnished with in America. To my mind it has a doubtful ring about it."

Streetcars were a form of transportation he never quite got the hang of, though. "Whenever you think you know where a car is

Horse-drawn streetcars at Potsdamer Platz, around 1900.

going to you would better stop ashore, because that car is not going to that place at all." The house numbers added to the confusion. "At first one thinks it was done by an idiot; but there is too much variety about it for that; an idiot could not think of so many different ways of making confusion and propagating blasphemy," Twain continued. "They often use one number for three or four houses. Sometimes they put a number on a house—4, for instance—then put 4a, 4b, 4c, on the succeeding houses, and one becomes old and decrepit before he finally arrives at 5.... But the worst feature of all this is that the numbers do not travel in any one direction, no, they travel along, then you perceive that the numbers are now traveling toward you from the opposite direction." This Berlin foible still drives visitors (and locals) crazy up to today. Twain was also flustered because he had to buy an additional ticket and present it for every mile. He often lost those tickets and had to pay twice, and was scolded by the conductor. To this day, Berlin streetcar conductors aren't known for their abundant friendliness.

The last horse car in Wedding. In 1901, streetcars began to run on gas.

Berlin was an adventure for the writer's daughters as well. The two older ones, Susy and Clara, dreamed about having musical careers. And it was common knowledge among the American upper classes that the best music education was available in Berlin, as Twain had already pointed out in his conversation with the *National-Zeitung*. Especially if someone were looking for a conservatory for musical instruments, Berlin would have been the inevitable choice. Soon Twain found such a school for his daughters, even fairly close to Körnerstrasse: The *American School for Young Girls*, founded in 1886, by Mary Bannister Willard. It was a boarding school, located at Nettelbeckstrasse in Schöneberg (replaced today by the street An der Urania, near Nollendorfplatz), right in the middle of what was already called the "American district" in the 1890s. Christopher Isherwood would later describe this neighborhood in his *Berlin Stories*, which inspired the musical *Cabaret*.

Mary Bannister Willard, who originally came from Fairfield, New York, was an outstanding emancipated woman for her time and

Nollendorfplatz around 1900. In the background is the former theater Neues Schauspielhaus. *To the right is the American church.*

age. After her husband passed away, she published the magazine of the WCTU, Woman's Christian Temperance Union. The WCTU was the largest women's organization in the United States, it advocated a number of social reform issues, including Prohibition. It endorsed the suffrage movement that fought for equal rights for women, and also did missionary work worldwide. Mary Willard went to Europe, presumably on assignment for the WCTU, taking her four children with her. She soon spotted a gap in Berlin's education market. There was no school for English-speaking girls, though quite a few of them lived in the city. So, Mary Willard started to offer the type of education that was deemed appropriate for young women, with an emphasis on the arts, music, German, and French. It was a unique, one-of-a-kind school, until 1891, when a branch was established in Paris. It is not clear whether Susy Clemens attended the school, but Clara definitely took music lessons there. The school advertised that it employed the best teachers available,

Moritz Moszkowski and Mary Bannister Willard, Clara's music teachers near Nollendorfplatz in Berlin.

and Clara received piano lessons from Moritz Moszkowski, a renowned concert pianist and composer with a large and impressive mustache, who was a member of the Berlin Academy of Arts.

Clara was a very strong-minded young woman, as the pianist would discover a few months later, when the Clemens family had left Berlin for Vienna and Clara stayed behind to complete her education, boarding with Mary Willard. The thirty-nine-year-old Moszkowski constantly wooed Twain's much younger daughter. Clara warned him that she would cancel the class if he did not stop pursuing her. Moszkowski, however, did not cease his behavior, so Clara abruptly stopped attending his lessons.

Twain already knew how stubborn his daughter could be—and also how attractive she was to young men. While Livy had searched for an apartment in Berlin in August 1891, Twain and his daughters had stayed in the spa at Marienbad. The seventeen-year-old beauty aroused quite a lot of attention in her new, low-cut dress. A group of young officers gathered around her, and one of the men exhibited an especially keen interest, until Twain reprimanded him sharply and banished Clara to her room. On a later occasion, Clara attended a ball held by the von Versens, where forty officers were present. Her father made it clear to her that a young American woman should not be alone in such company, but she went anyway. Her nineteen-year-old sister, Susy, was much shyer; she relied on family friends from the American embassy to navigate Berlin's social scene, especially on Theodore Bingham, the ambassador's attaché. "He never left me sitting alone," Twain's biographer Bigelow Paine noted, "nor in an awkward situation of any kind, but always came cordially to the rescue. My gratitude toward him was absolutely limitless."

Susy and Clara had a great time at festivities and dinner parties, and they loved to be in their father's limelight. "Susy and I felt proud to be his daughters," Clara wrote in her memoirs. "In fact, with satisfied vanity we enjoyed watching people point out our family when we entered a dining-room. At first we pretended to be indifferent to the visible attention we attracted, but at last my sister and I confessed to each other that it must be queer to belong to a family in which no one was distinguished or famous."

But they also felt a constant pressure to be as brilliant as their dad, as Clara remembered as well. Twain was, "thanks to no violent physical effort on his part, wonderfully popular in Berlin," she told *The New York Times* in June 1908, after the family had already returned to New York. "When I was not studying hard at my music, I would go out occasionally to little functions, where I would sit in a corner and be completely ignored by all assembled until some foolish person whispered to another: 'I believe that's Mark Twain's daughter in the corner.' Then the guests would arise as one man and swoop down upon me, and expect me to be 'bright' and amusing after a hard day's work." But that only happened on the "occasions when my august parent was not present. At social gatherings graced by his presence, however, my existence was on the level of a footstool—always an unnecessary object in a crowded room. Father, fresh from bed, would completely flood the place with his talk."

But despite those quibbles, the family spent a lot of time together. Once, they visited the Salamonski Circus. At first, they had fun, but then they witnessed a terrible accident involving a girl of sixteen or seventeen riding a horse, according to Henry Fisher. "While she was doing a *salto mortale*, a clown ran in and dived between the horse's legs. The horse got frightened and threw the rider." Twain's daughters laughed, but Twain said, "Keep still, children, don't you see the poor girl is hurt?" When the family was about to leave, a "gypsy-looking, elderly woman came running from behind the scenes, looking about wildly. When her eye located the clown, she rushed up to him and hit him a terrible blow in the face. 'You have ruined my girl. She will never be able to ride again,' she cried. 'Served him right,' said Twain. 'I do hope the manager gets a clout on the jaw, too. For he really is the responsible guy. The clown has to get laughs, the girl has to risk her limbs, so that the manager may coin money.'"

According to his diary, Twain also occasionally met friends to play cards in the café at the Hotel de Rome on Unter den Linden. And he and Olivia went to the theater or concerts quite often. They watched a performance of Mozart's *Don Giovanni*, as well as Goethe's play, *Götz von Berlichingen*. Twain not only watched the play, he bought the script and studied it thoroughly beforehand. The play is quite famous in Germany, because Götz, a count, tells Kaiser Maximilian that he could kiss his ass.

After one of those nights out, however, Twain found himself locked out of his apartment—again. It was customary in Berlin for tenements to be locked at 10 p.m. sharp, so tenants had to carry their keys. Twain was either not aware of that, or he just forgot his keys quite often. In those cases, he had no choice but to ring the bell and wake up the porter. A Berlin porter was something between a handyman and a doorman. He watched the door and made sure no one messed with anything. He also made small repairs, if he felt like it. Porters typically lived on the ground floor, or in the basement. Like streetcar conductors, they were not known for being beacons of cheerfulness, pretty much like most native Berliners, especially blue-collar folks. Pastor Dickie had advised his compatriots to stay on the good side of their porters, because everybody would need their services eventually. And the best way to do so, Dickie pointed out, was to slip them a dollar every month.

When Twain arrived at his apartment in the middle of the night without a key once again, he anticipated who would stand before him: a disgruntled porter who would first make him wait and then berate him with slurs and insults. To his huge surprise, the situation panned out completely differently. The man welcomed him joyfully, saying, "You are Mark Twain—I just learned that today!" Evidently the porter had only known the tenant by his actual name, Samuel Clemens. The porter went on to remark enthusiastically that he had read all of Twain's books, and that Huckleberry Finn was his favorite fictional character. After the porter realized who Twain was, the author could have come home whenever he wished and never bothered with the keys, though from then on, he always carried them with him.

While the incident itself is not much disputed, it is not clear when or where it took place. Dickie believes that the "lock out" happened on Körnerstrasse, but he also writes that Twain was coming home from a dinner with the Kaiser. That dinner took place in February, however, when the Clemens family was living in the Hotel Royal, the much fancier place they moved to on New Year's Eve 1891. Bigelow Paine describes the same episode. He not only places it in the Hotel Royal, he also claims it actually happened in February.

Twain himself related the incident to Paine in 1907, without being specific about the date, but he also claimed that it happened after his dinner with the Kaiser. The porter was a "tow-headed young German, twenty-two or twenty-three years old; and it had been for some time apparent to me that he did not enjoy being hammered out of his sleep nights to let me in. He never had a kind word for it, nor a pleasant look. I couldn't understand it, since it was his business to be on watch and let the occupants of the several flats in at any and all hours of the night." However, there was a "custom, which was so well established and so universally recognized that it had all the force and dignity of law."

By authority of this custom, "whosoever entered a Berlin house after ten at night must pay a trifling toll to the porter for breaking his sleep to let him in. This tax was either two and a half cents, or five cents, I don't remember which; but I had never paid it, and didn't even know about it." On that very night, Twain, arrived "sorrowful and anxious," awaiting an "indignant face, a resentful face, the face of the porter," and prepared to wait for the usual "tedious minute or two" to be let in. But instead, "the door was instantly unlocked, unbolted, unchained, and flung wide," and he was greeted by the porter's round face, "all sunshine and smiles and welcome," who poured out a "generous stream of German welcome and homage, meanwhile dragging me excitedly to his small bedroom beside the front door, there he made me bend down over a row of German translations of my books and said, 'There! You wrote them! I have found it out! By God! I did not know it before, and I ask a million pardons!'"

The porter then told him that his favorite book was *Old Times on the Mississippi,* the same book the Kaiser liked best. Twain saw this as a coincidence that overshadowed all other coincidences for its "picturesque-ness." However, the reason Twain believed that the incident happened after the dinner with the Kaiser is probably just that it improved upon the story. In reality, it sounds much more like a scene in a tenement than in an upscale hotel. Also, it would probably not have taken him weeks to figure out that he had to tip a hotel bellboy. But evidently, this is one of those events that are difficult to reconstruct after such a long time.

Twain was invited to give quite a few lectures in Berlin, and one of his favorite topics was the German language. He had published an essay, "The Awful German Language," about eleven years prior (in the appendix of *A Tramp Abroad),* after his first trip to Germany. And he continued to collect linguistic accidents, such as *Nachfragestellenanknote,* or *Stückholzer,* but also actual German expressions like *Weltanschauung* (philosophy of life) or *Gesegnete Mahlzeit* (blessed meal). He was sure about one thing: "No foreigner can read it, unless maybe the Creator, but certainly no other." He also noted in his diary, "Those people are so fond of the parenthesis in their speech that children inherit it in their bodies—look at

The site of the former English House at 49 Mohrenstrasse—more of an American place today. Also, the whole block is brand new.

those bow-legged children over there." Another one of his quips was, "Wouldn't be as lonesome as a G[erman] verb for anything in the world." (In German, verbs are placed at the end of a sentence, far apart from the subject.) Once, he rode a streetcar with Henry Fisher, and a woman with especially large breasts sat on a bench across from them. Twain, who was marveling at the size of them, curiously asked if "bosom" were masculine, feminine, or neutral. When Fisher revealed that it was masculine, *der Busen,* Twain laughed so hard he started to cry.

On Thanksgiving—November 26, 1891—he was asked by the American Physicians' Association to lecture to about two hundred guests, mostly doctors, as the *Chicago Daily Tribune* reported the following day. He spoke at the English House at 49 Mohrenstrasse, near the Gendarmenmarkt, a neoclassical plaza with the Royal Theater (today the Berlin Concert Hall), and the German and French

Gendarmenmarkt with the German and the French Cathedrals and the Royal Concert Hall, in 1900. The plaza was rebuilt after World War II.

Cathedrals. The English House was one of the oldest artists' cafés in Berlin, and had been a meeting place for various art organizations since the 18th century.

The *Liedertafel* choir met there, as well as the Berlin Artist Association and the avant-garde literary society *Tunnel über der Spree* ("tunnel over the Spree River"), an organization once described by a rather snarky member as a "daycare center for smalltime authors." Twain made extensive notes in his diary for his Thanksgiving Day speech, so we have an idea of what he talked about. "Glad to see so many faces—they call up our home over the sea—when you are a stranger in a strange land & the face of a countryman comes before you it summons land & country," he started. "Not that G[ermany] isn't home to us—They treat us well. And we came originally from G[ermany]—& we should be dumb without the G[erman] words in our lang." He went on to say that he was glad to see all these doctors, the "highest of all professions—the stilling of human pain, the saving of human life." Of course, even the doctors were targets of his mild fun, "A half-educated physician is not valuable. He thinks he can cure everything—cancer, stammering, idiocy—there isn't anything he won't undertake—& there is just where he is so dangerous. If he knew more he would undertake less, & the undertaker would have a rest." But he mostly talked about Berlin. "Without a doubt Berlin is the place to come to finish your medical education. For certainly it is a luminous centre of intelligence—a place where the last possibilities of attainment in all the sciences are to be had for the seeking. Berlin is a wonderful city for that sort of opportunity. They teach everything here. I don't believe there is anything in the whole earth that you can't learn in Berlin except the German language."

Now on topic, he continued, "It is a desperate language. They think it is the language of concentration. They hitch a cattle-train of words together & vestibule it, & because there isn't a break in it from one end to the other they think that is concentration & and they call it so. An officer gave me this word the other day—got it out of a navel handbook: 'Marine-intendant-undersecretariats-applicant.' Great SCOTT! There are 41 letters in that word. It merely concentrates the alphabet—with a shovel." He went on to say, "I wrote a chapter on this language [i.e. the essay on the 'Awful German Language'] 13 years ago & tried my level best to improve it & simplify it for these people—& this is the result. It hurts me to know that that chapter is not in any of their text books & they don't use it in the University. If I could get an imperial decree it would help the reform along." And then Twain, in traditional American fashion, summed it up, "But the fact is, they ought to adapt our language. It is so simple & easy & whereas."

Twain got a lot of applause, but he fretted in a letter to Frederick Hall one day later that "when they threw my portrait on a screen it was a sorrowful reminder, for it was from a negative of 15 years ago & hadn't a grey hair in it." (He had just sent a letter to Franklin G. Whitmore, asking for a new photograph of himself, as well as for autograph cards.) After the lecture, Twain joined his acquaintances from the embassy, William Walter Phelps and his daughter Marian, Fritz von Rottenburg, Theodore Bingham, and also Chapman Coleman, the managing secretary who ran the place. They attended a Thanksgiving banquet at the *Kaiserhof* on Mohrenstrasse.

In those days, Twain also finally received some good news from New York. In a letter to Hall, he thanked his publisher for the last royalty statement, which was "really enlightening & satisfactory," and made him feel a "great let-up from depression," since "everything looks so fine & handsome with the business now." He also wrote that his arm was "so much better now." He had "stolen a couple of days & finished-up a couple of McClure letters that have been lying a long time." These letters were about his visits to Marienbad and Switzerland, the latter including a description of the Swiss mountain Jungfrau. "I shall write the 6th & last letter by & by when I have studied Berlin sufficiently." He signs off in a "most cheerful frame of mind." He also takes the time to answer an acquaintance's questions about the book, *Nights with Uncle Remus*, a collection of African-American folk tales by Joel Chandler Harris, an author from Atlanta, Georgia.

The Clemenses were frequently invited to the famed Berlin salons of that era, regular get-togethers of artists and intellectuals at someone's home. On December 1, Olivia wrote a letter to George H. Warner, a former neighbor in Hartford, Connecticut,—occasionally she took over her husband's correspondence, due to his rheumatism—and she gushed, "Berlin is a most interesting city and the people *charming.*" She had just returned from a lecture on German literature by a "German lady professor who I think is one of the most intellectual women that I have ever met," she continued. Olivia was taking German lessons from her. She also had met a couple "Mr. and Mrs. du Bois Raymond," that was "most delightful . . . full of interest in everything," and who were "descendants of Mendelssohn." Olivia was referring to Moses Mendelssohn, a famed 18th century philosopher, who was an early proponent of Enlightenment and Reform Judaism. "His father is one of the great and learned scientists here, and her father is [Sebastian] Hensel,"

The interior of the former Mendelssohn bank at Jaegerstrasse, next to the then-residence. Now, it houses a small museum devoted to the family.

Olivia added. She ended her letter to Warner with: "Susy thinks Berlin is too gray but I think she likes it better than she did at first."

The couple Olivia was writing about was Lili Hensel and her husband, Alard Du Bois-Reymond [not Raymond], a professor of Latin and Greek. Alard was the son of Emil Du Bois Reymond, a university doctor and descendant of Huguenots. Emil Du Bois is regarded as the father of experimental electrophysiology. Lili's father was, in fact, Sebastian Hensel, known today as the chronicler of the widespread Mendelssohn family. But his main occupation was real estate. He was the founding director of the Hotel Kaiserhof in 1875. In the 1880s, the city of Berlin commissioned him to develop fifteen indoor markets modeled on Les Halles in Paris.

Sebastian was the son of Fanny Hensel, the sister of the famed 19th-century composer Felix Mendelssohn-Bartholdy. Fanny had as much musical talent as her brother, Felix, but in those times, women were barred from pursuing careers in the public eye, es-

Above: The Mendelssohn family plot at the Dreifaltigkeits-kirchhof in Kreuzberg. Left, Felix Mendelssohn-Bartholdy, right, his sister Fanny Hensel.

Below: The grave of the Du Bois family at the Französischer Friedhof (French cemetery) at Chausseestrasse, in Mitte. Many Huguenots are buried here.

pecially if they came from a family like the Mendelssohns, who were bankers and the third-richest Jewish family in Germany. In 1890, the Mendelssohn banking house was located at 51 Jägerstrasse near the Gendarmenmarkt, right next to the family residence, Palais Mendelssohn. Hermann von Helmholtz and his wife, Anna, were frequent guests at Jaegerstrasse, as was Theodor Mommsen. We don't know for sure, but it is very likely that the Clemenses attended a dinner party or salon at 53 Jaegerstrasse at some point.

Rudolf Lindau, Bismarck's press secretary in Paris, who was also a world traveler and a fiction writer, became one of Mark Twain's best friends in Berlin and later-on.

One of Sebastian Hensel's cousins living at Jaegerstrasse was Ernst von Mendelssohn-Bartholdy. He was an ally of Bismarck and helped finance the Iron Chancellor's private (and public) expenses. Ernst von Mendelssohn visited the United States shortly after the Civil War. In 1869, he wrote a book about his trip in which he remarked that the co-existence of black and white folks in America was difficult and might not work out in the long run.

The Clemenses also visited another couple, Heinrich and Elisabeth Nelson, a lawyer and a painter, who maintained their salon not in Mitte, but in Klopstockstrasse, in the lofty district of Charlottenburg (Twain noted their address in his diary). They were also descendants of Moses Mendelssohn. Later, their son Leonard Nelson founded the International Socialist Combat League. Eventually, the League became a resistance group against the Nazis. Around that time, Twain met a man who became one of his closest friends in Berlin, and later in Vienna, and even in New York: Rudolf Lindau, then a sixty-two-year-old diplomat and also a novelist. Twain

Potsdamer Strasse in the 1890s. Lindau lived around the corner.

would soon call him "Rudolf the incomparable" and "one of the head saints in this family's calendar."

Lindau led a life full of unrest, and of writing, much like Twain himself. Born in 1829 in Gardelegen, a village near Berlin, to a lawyer of Jewish faith and the daughter of a pastor, he spent part of his youth at the Lycée Bonaparte in Paris, studying literature. He kept returning to Paris (and France in general) time and again. But he also traveled to Italy, England, and the Netherlands. In 1860, he left Marseille for East Asia via Egypt, Ceylon, Singapore, and Hong Kong, by ship and train, quite an unusual journey at that time. From Shanghai, he went to Japan, traveling frequently between Yokohama, Nagasaki, and Yedo, known today as Tokyo.

Lindau was assigned as the consul of Switzerland to close a business agreement between the Swiss and the Japanese governments. Those were exciting years: He witnessed the murder of two ship captains and the execution of pirates, and he survived a rebel attack on Shanghai. He also traveled to Saigon, Macao, and Vladivostok, and, supposedly, California. And he did consulting work for a few American companies. Later, he co-founded two English-language papers, Japan Punch and the Japan Times.

After ten years in the Far East, Lindau went back to Paris via California and New York, riding the new intercontinental railway. At first, he wrote travel novels. In 1873, he became Bismarck's press secretary in the French capital, in charge of easing the anti-German attitude of the French press. But he always had a somewhat tense relationship with the Iron Chancellor. The latter didn't entirely trust him, due to his unconventional biography. Lindau went back to Berlin in 1878, and continued to work as Bismarck's press secretary; the rather conservative official was mostly trying to undermine the liberal German press. After Bismarck's fall two years later, Lindau stayed on at the Foreign Office and kept in close contact with wheelers and dealers such as Bismarck's son, Herbert, a member of the Reichstag, or Gerson von Bleichröder, the richest man in Prussia, also of German-Jewish heritage, who was nicknamed "Bismarck's banker." Bleichröder had negotiated the French reparation payments of 1871, which in turn had fueled the industrial boom in Berlin that Twain admired so much.

But Lindau's heart always belonged to literature. He wrote more than a dozen novels in German, as well as in French and English—his British publishers were William and John Blackwood from Scotland. And he corresponded with many fellow writers, such as Theodor Fontane and Hermann Sudermann. We don't know how Twain met Lindau, but it was most likely Lindau who approached the American, who, at that time, must have been more famous in Berlin than Ernest Hemingway in Paris. Twain's first letter to Lindau is from December 7, 1891, in which he responds to a suggestion to meet. "I am delighted and beg to name Wednesday, as that is the only unengaged evening I have this week." Four days later, he thanked Lindau for a dinner in the latter's home at Sigismundstrasse (west of Potsdamer Strasse) that was "too delicious & too exquisite in every way for mere sinful human beings," and continued, "All through, it was an ideal evening, in ideal quarters, with ideal helps of all kinds to make it perfect."

He also announced that he had "soaked an old cob pipe in whisky all the morning, for you." And in an undated letter, presumably from the same week, he wrote, "Yes, time is flying—let us be old friends right away! I'm with you there, and thank you for suggesting it." He went on to relate many details from his life, as his new "old friend" had asked, such as how he managed to win the hand of Olivia, even though he was "poor & totally unknown" then and the Langdons were the most important family in town. "I staid several weeks & persecuted the girl & got refused twice, & was finally accepted, the girl being tired out."

Later in his life, Twain pondered to write about Lindau, but he did not want to disclose his friend's name, so he named Lindau "Smith," in his dictations. "'Smith' was a special friend of mine," he told Bigelow Paine, his biographer, "I greatly enjoyed his society, although in order to have it, it was necessary for me to seek it as late as midnight." Such high-ranking bureaucrats as Lindau, Twain pointed out, worked all day after nine in the morning, and then attended official banquets in the evening. So they were unable to get some "life-restoring fresh air and exercise for their jaded minds and bodies earlier than midnight." They turned out afterward and "gratefully and violently tramped the deserted streets until two in the morning." Those two must have had interesting conversations in Berlin, but sadly, no records of them were preserved.

Twain also told Lindau in one of his letters that Ambassador Phelps had organized a reading in Dresden, about one hundred miles south of Berlin, on December 18. It was at a dinner held by the English and American Club. "I told him I would read if he would go with me & keep me from getting lost on the way—so I suppose he is going." (Phelps went.) Twain read a satirical piece about the French duel from *A Tramp Abroad*, where the biggest danger is that the combatants could catch a cold in the open air, and the folk tale "Tar Baby," and possibly something about Oudinot, a fictional character from Kentucky and a compulsive liar. And, of course, he spoke about his favorite topic, "The Horrors of the German language." According to *The New York Times*, he suggested either reforming it or putting it "in the lumber room of dead ancient languages." He ended the evening with "Ghost Story." The following week, Twain asked a friend in Dresden to send him two clippings from local newspapers about the event. After his death, the letter was auctioned off for a lot of money, which the author surely could have used himself!

Twain went mostly because he desperately needed the money he would get for the lecture. His funds were drying up faster than he had expected, because Berlin was not as cheap as Twain, like many Americans before and after him, had hoped. Pastor James Dickie met quite a few college students who found themselves in financial hardship because their expenses had gotten out of hand. For instance, a steak in Berlin cost forty cents a pound at the time, pretty much the same amount one would pay in America then. Dickie himself once said that he was spending as much money in Berlin for everyday expenses as he would have in his native Detroit.

In addition, Twain was faced with paying taxes. When Max Horwitz from the *National-Zeitung* asked Twain how long he planned on staying in Berlin, he replied, "Until your taxes will drive me out again." Germany had just passed a law to tax foreigners at a rate of five percent of their income, starting in January 1892. This was to the chagrin of many Americans, including Twain. Germany should not tax a foreigner, who is "neither a nuisance, nor does he wish to become one," he said to Horwitz. Instead, Berlin should tax dogs. Actually, Berlin does tax dogs these days, but not visitors, so Twain did have some impact!

At first, he didn't care that much, as long as the Prussians only estimated his income. "I don't mind lying about little things like that," he told Fisher. "On the contrary, making a clean breast of it, I confessed that I get a whole cent a word for every word I do, even for little words like 'I' or 'Manafraidofhismotherinlaw.' Did they believe me? Not they! They thought I was exaggerating." But the Prussian authorities never forgot someone they had registered, especially not if he owed them money. On December 1, 1891, Twain's tax assessment was delivered to Körnerstrasse—a document discovered by Albert Locher, a contemporary Swiss literary scholar, and published in his book *Mit Mark Twain durch Europa* (Touring

Europe with Mark Twain). The bill states that forty-eight marks and forty pennies were due. To put this into perspective, one could stay in a high-end hotel for a week for that amount of money in 1981. Twain did not react, let alone actually pay taxes, so he received a reminder in the mail four weeks later.

But the writer really started to complain when the Prussian authorities asked for an additional amount of twelve marks in church taxes. He told them that he had gone to church only once—and that he couldn't possibly afford a second visit. He found the very idea of a church tax outrageous. "Only the rich can be saved here," he wrote in his diary. However, Pastor Dickie confirmed in his book that Twain had, in fact, attended mass a few times after all, so the writer was only flexing his sarcastic muscle. It was probably his wife, Livy, who dragged him to the service, a "beautiful soul," as Dickie recalls, whose "memory was very sweetly cherished by the ladies of the Berlin Church."

On December 22, Twain sent a long letter to Frederick Hall (against Livy's advice), in which he not only complained about the "eternal German tax gatherer," he also blamed Edmund Clarence Stedman for his lack of funds. Stedman was the editor of the *Library of American Literature,* published under his Webster brand. He felt that Stedman had taken advantage of the "deranged" Charles Webster and was getting a huge sum of royalties for books that were not making any money, while Twain himself was cash-strapped. He went so far to call Stedman a "cold-blooded shark." Hall, however, tried to assuage Twain's money woes by explaining that "McClure is paying very slowly . . . Of course we are perfectly secure since the contract is guaranteed by the 'N.Y. Sun.'" Eventually, Hall would consider bypassing McClure and ask the *New York Sun* directly for money. But for now, Olivia asked Hall to send a new "letter of credit for ten thousand dollars dated about Feb 1st 1892 and to run a year." The Clemenses had such a letter of credit when they arrived in Berlin, but it was due to run out in January 1892. The new money came from Olivia's wealthy brother, Charles Langdon. She was planning to withdraw a thousand dollars per month, even though she'd "hate to use it because it is *principal* that has fallen in

Slovenly Peter, *Twain's favorite children's book, known in Germany as* Struwwelpeter. *He translated the book as a Christmas gift to his own children, hut he was unable to publish the book in America.*

and not interest." She also encouraged Hall to send more letters, which had a calming influence on her "restless" husband.

A little subdued, but determined to keep their spirits up, the family celebrated Christmas at Körnerstrasse. And Twain had a special gift for his daughters. "Under the Christmas tree that year, with its shining silver and gold and its yellow candles, the little girls found the translation of *Struwwelpeter*," *The New York Times* reported. Twain had "wrapped it up himself, twining a large red ribbon around it as an ornament. Seated by the tree, he read the verses aloud so dramatically that his audience of three was moved to tears and laughter." He also sent his best Christmas wishes to Lindau, Phelps, and Mary Willard, his daughter Clara's music teacher. Willard also got a signed copy of his book, *A Connecticut Yankee in King Arthur's Court*, whereas Lindau got a picture of Twain—nearly eight years old, "but it is the last that was taken," Twain wrote, asking for a picture of his friend in return. He also sent a letter to Hall that was somewhat less festive. He wrote in capitals, "PLEASE RENEW MY LETTER OF CREDIT," and added, "Expires Jan. 7."

But despite his monetary problems, and even though he had paid the rent in advance, Twain left his tenement at the end of the year. According to his diary, he had made the decision on December 12, and he even retained a lawyer to speed things up. "It's all up with Körnerstrasse, too much police," Twain said to Fisher. Fisher described two events, and it was the second run-in that tipped the scale. The first confrontation took place when a policeman stormed the apartment on a charge of "public enragement." The officer claimed that he could see the Clemenses' bed linen through their window from the street level, although only when he stood on his toes. Twain did not give the policeman the respect the latter demanded upon entering. Grumbling at the intrusion, he remarked, "I haven't had any breakfast, and if the Kaiser himself called, I would throw him out." Having insulted an official, Twain had to appear in court and pay a fifty-mark fine, wrote Fisher. Twenty marks were for disorderly conduct in the courtroom, because Twain had casually crossed his legs. He also paid ten marks for showcasing his bedding, and another twenty for laughing at the police officer.

The veracity of this story, however, is rather questionable. First of all, Twain did not mention this occurrence in his diary, nor did he tell Bigelow Paine about it. It was also impossible to look into a second-floor window. And last, but not least, Fisher's book was published shortly after World War I, when America was hit by a wave of anti-German sentiment. It is very likely that Fisher put words into Twain's mouth, to make Germany look bad.

There was, however, a second, less disputed visit from the police that ultimately ticked Twain off. The police had told him that he, as the head of the household, was responsible for supervising all of the people living in the apartment, including the help. So Twain was asked by a policeman whether he was certain that his maids had been vaccinated against smallpox. Twain assured him that he did not know, and that he had never seen any vaccination scars. When the policeman suggested that they could have vaccination scars hidden on their legs—since "some women were so vain," Twain replied, "Possibly, but I have looked neither under their arms nor under their petticoats—I presume they have legs. However, I don't know anything about them, for sure. And this being their day out, if you *must* investigate, they will be back about ten o'clock, and, returning, you may look for yourself, if the law says so." According to Fisher, Twain continued, "That policeman did return and told the girls that he was authorized by me to look for their vaccination marks, wherever located. Of course, it caused a row all around, the girls protesting that I was no gentleman. So, to end it all, I paid the rent for the whole year, eleven months' rent, and left the flat."

While this story has a true core, it is most likely an embellishment. The Prussian police had, in fact, every conceivable authority, but whether or not they reached under the skirt of a maid is rather questionable. The culture was far too prudish at the time. But Prussians were not shy about their veneration of the uniform. This utmost respect for authority, uniforms, and blind obedience to the police and the military, however, was foreign to Twain. So it's understandable that he often clashed with the police, though the details passed down might have been exaggerated over time.

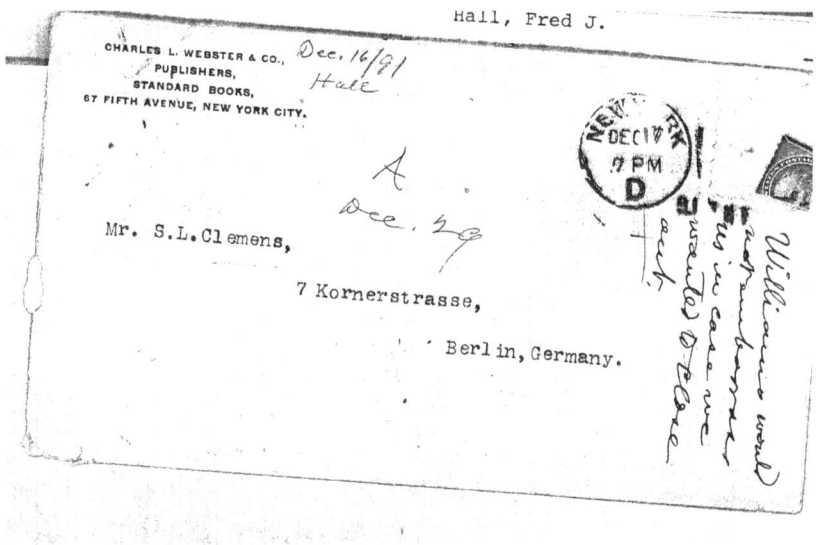

The last letter Webster publisher Frederick Hall sent to Körnerstrasse.

Twain wrote a letter to the realtor, Mr. Prächtel, to ask him to take back the furniture and to tell him that he would pay for "some trifles of crockery" and two windows that were broken. He also reminded him that the landlord, Rittmeister Killisch, would have to consent to any new tenant moving in. Maybe Twain was trying to find somebody who was willing to take over his lease. And he asked the realtor to give the house key to Fritz, the porter, his new (and already lost) friend. He also expressed hefty discontent in his diary. He felt that Prächtel had taken "advantage of our ignorance to charge us four prices. That was your turn. Mine is coming. I have no recourse against you except with printer's ink, but dear sir I will see to it that you have barrels of that." He was referring, of course, to "On Renting a Flat in Berlin," which, alas, did not see the light of day up to now. But at least his remarks about the German stove were published, though only long after his death as well, in his story "Conversations with Satan."

The famed tiled stove from the Napoleonic era in Zur letzten Instanz (Court of Last Resort), the oldest pub in Berlin, founded at Waisenstrasse in 1621. Mark Twain might or might not have been here.

A Reflection on the German Stove
From: Conversations with Satan

By Mark Twain

I had that glimpse of Satan and his shadow, and the next moment he was by my side in the room. He did not embarrass me. Real royalties do not embarrass one; they are sure of their place, sure of its recognition; and so they bear about with them an alpine serenity and reposefulness which quiet the nerves of the spectator. It is the prerogative of a viscount or a baron to make a person feel small, and of a baronet to extinguish him.

(...)

In Germany the sofa is the seat of honor and is always offered to the guest. It may be so in Austria also, therefore I tendered it to Satan, and called him by the loftiest titles I could think of — Durchlauschtigst, and Ihro Majestät — but he declined it, saying he would have no ceremony, and so took a chair. He said —

"You are very comfortable here. The German stove is the best in the universe."

"I agree to that, with all my heart, Durchlauscht. That one there is eleven feet high and four feet square, and looks like a graveyard monument built of white tiles; but its looks are its only blemish. At eight in the morning it burns up one small basketful of wood in twenty minutes, and that is all it requires for the day. This great room will keep the same level and pleasant and comfortable degree of warmth hour after hour without change, and there is no artificial heat in the world that is comparable to it for wholesomeness, healthfulness. It does not inflame the skin, it does not oppress the head or make the temples throb; there isn't a headache in a hundred years of it. As for economy, it is a good ten times more economical than any other house-heating apparatus known to the world."

"You use it in America, of course?"

I was pleasantly surprised at that, and said—

"Is it possible that Ihro Majestät is not familiar with America?"

"Well—no. I have not been there lately. I am not needed there."

At first I was gratified; but next I was suspicious that maybe his remark did not quite mean what I had thought it meant; so it seemed good diplomacy not to stir the matter, but leave it alone and go on about the stove again.

"No," I said, "we don't use the German stove in America. We have the name of being the most ingenious of the nations in the matter of inventing and putting to practical use all manner of conveniences, comforts, and labor-saving and money-saving contrivances, and we have fairly earned that name and are proud of it; but we do not know how to heat a house rationally, yet, and it seems likely that we shall never learn. The most of our stoves are extravagant wasters of fuel; the most of them require frequent attention and recharging; none of them furnishes a continuously equable heat, and we have not one that does not scorch the skin and oppress the head. We have spent tons and tons of money upon furnaces with elaborate and costly arrangements for distributing dry heat or steam or hot water throughout a house; but they are all ravenous coal-cannibals, and if there is one among them whose heat-output can be successfully regulated I have not seen it. As far as my knowledge goes, we have none but insane ways of heating houses and railway cars in America."

"Then why don't you introduce the German stove?"

"I wish I could. I could save the country money enough annually to pay the silly pension bill. And if we had that admirable stove we should soon find a way to rid it of its grim and ghostly look and make it a pretty and graceful thing to look at, and an ornament to the room; for we are a capable people in those directions. But I suppose we shall never see the day. The Americans who come over here do not study the German stove, they merely make fun of its personal appearance, and go away without finding out what a competent and inexpensive miracle it is. The Berlin stove is the best that I have seen. When we kept house there several winters ago we charged our parlor monument at 7 in the morning with a peck of cheap briquettes made of refuse coal-dust, let the fire burn half an hour, then shut up the stove and never touched it again for twenty-four hours. All day long and up to past midnight that room was perfectly comfortable, not too hot, not too cold, and the heat not varying, but remaining at the same pleasant level all the time. Do you like the German stove, Durchlauscht?"

"Not for my boarders—no."

"What do you use, Durchlauscht?"

He named sixty-four varieties of stoves and house-furnaces. Dear me, those old familiar names—they were all American! But I didn't say anything. I was ashamed; and yet at the same time I was conscious of a private little thrill of patriotic pride in the reflection that in a humble way we had been able to add a discomfort to hell.

The Hotel Royal at Unter den Linden and Wilhelmstrasse at 1890.

Twain rented an eight-room suite in the Hotel Royal at 3 Unter den Linden—six bedchambers, one dining room, and one parlor—where the family arrived on December 31, at 1:30 p.m. He sent an advance note, asking for more blankets, a soft bed in the parents' bedroom, and a "secretary, a wardrobe & bureau" in every bedroom. The Royal was an older building, with a ground floor and two upper stories, located at the southeast corner of Unter den Linden and Wilhelmstrasse, close to the Brandenburg Gate.

A few years later, the famous Hotel Adlon would be built on the southwest corner of Wilhelmstrasse, directly on Pariser Platz, next to where the American embassy would relocate in the 1930s. The Adlon and the embassy were destroyed during World War II; only after the Berlin Wall came down was a new hotel built there, modeled after the original (as well as a new embassy). East of the Royal, at 5 Unter den Linden, next to the Russian embassy, the Hotel Bristol opened in 1892. Naturally, the Bristol was a much more modern establishment, with ten apartments and an elevator, com-

The site of the Royal today. This building houses Bundestag *offices.*

plete with bathing facilities. Newspaper ads claimed that the Bristol was a first-class hotel, with electricity rather than gas lamps. But the Hotel Royal was substantially cheaper, and Twain (or, more likely, Olivia) had not given up completely on saving money. The Royal was built in the 18th century and had been modernized in 1860, although it did not have an elevator. But it had only two floors. And it flourished nonetheless, because of its excellent reputation and location. Ambassadors and crowned heads of state had resided there, and it was called "noble" in *Baedeker's* guidebook. The Royal only served wine; beer was not permitted, because it was deemed vulgar.

Most importantly, the Hotel Royal offered a fabulous view of the royal boulevard Unter den Linden, the Brandenburg Gate, and the palaces, fountains, and gardens on Pariser Platz. It was a much more appropriate address for a distinguished American writer than a tenement. Besides, many of Twain's friends—the von Versens, Phelps, Coleman—lived just around the corner. By the second day, Twain and Olivia had been invited by Secretary

The Brandenburg Gate around 1890, as Twain saw it from his hotel window. The Victory column is in the background.

John Jackson from the embassy (as *The New York Times* duly reported). The Clemenses were accompanied by fellow correspondent Murat Halstead and his wife.

Clara Clemens recalls in her biography that she felt "perfectly happy" in their new home. She would often stand at the window and watch the emperor, Kaiser Wilhelm II, and his entourage leave every morning from the castle, ride along the Linden, and then exit through the Brandenburg Gate into the Tiergarten, Berlin's central park, and a former forest and hunting ground. Clara, who was inspired by this sight, wrote that the emperor "was a most romantic and brilliant figure, and we never tire of hearing stories about him." Unter den Linden was nearly two hundred feet wide; it was three streets in one, as Twain described it, with the famous linden trees and a bridle path in the middle for horse-drawn carriages. Twain referred to this middle strip, where only the Kaiser was allowed to

The Brandenburg Gate today. The plaza has been completely rebuilt. The Victory column with the angel was moved into the Tiergarten.

ride, as the "Holy Land." He often observed His Majesty in a carriage, drawn by his nobly-bred horses. Twain wrote in his notes that "all the horses seem to be of very fine breed; though I am not an expert in horses & do not speak with assurance. I can always tell which is the front end of a horse, but beyond that my art is not above the ordinary."

Also Jean, his youngest daughter, was thrilled and awed. "The Emperor drives up and down Unter den Linden," she wrote in her diary. "The people wait in lines for the Emperor. The Emperor is one of the handsomest men I have ever seen. He bows or salutes with great dignity to the crowds that wait his arrival. He has five sons and there was a report that he had six." (According to Fisher, Twain once remarked that the Kaiser had an affair with the wife of the French ambassador, so maybe that's where Jean got that idea.) She also liked the Tiergarten. "The Thiergarten is a pleasure resort,

An ad in a Berlin paper for the new Hotel Bristol, next to the Royal.

it is a big wood with very good walks and drives through it," she wrote. "There are also little lakes, which are covered in summer and fall with ducks and swans, in winter with skating boys and girls." She also went to school, "for the first time in my life, and have enjoyed it very much. I fed two horses every morning on my way to school, one of which wanted to follow me one morning."

Clara mostly loved the Hotel Royal itself. "Now and then arrangements were made for private meals when we met with a hotel manager particularly anxious to show his gratitude for our stopping in his hotel," she wrote. "But Susy and I greatly preferred the public dining-room where we could examine interesting types." She continues to describe an incident when both girls saw a "most distinguished-looking man" in the dining room. They began to obsess "over his fine brow, classic features, Grecian figure, and spiritual smile." Finally, Twain introduced himself to the man, who was British. Sadly, the Englishman refused to believe that his *vis-à-vis* was the famous American writer Mark Twain. So, this went no-

The monument for Frederick the Great, still at Unter den Linden.

where. "After that, my sister and I kept very quiet about our ideals discovered on European travels," wrote Clara. Also Susan Crane, Olivia's older, adopted sister, was relieved to be staying in an upscale hotel, since she did not speak German. According to Albert Locher, a young waiter named Ernst Köppe served as her personal interpreter from then on. She was so thankful that she invited him to Elmira, New York; and he, in fact, visited her later.

Twain began to explore the neighborhood. Unter den Linden had—and has—many famous buildings, including the Palace of the Crown Prince, the Royal Opera, and the Friedrichs Wilhelm's University, as well as the Café Bauer at Friedrichstrasse, and the Hotel de Rome, next to the bronze monument for Frederick the Great, who governed Prussia in the 18th century.

Twain was quite fond of the Frederick statue, but he hated the golden victory angel in front of the Reichstag then. "Berlin has no public buildings that are majestic enough to comport with the universal stateliness of the city or furnish it with points of emphasis.

Except the statue of Frederick the Great, & one other memorial, its monuments are not of a prominent or insistent sort," he wrote in a story titled "The Postal Service," which, for whatever reason, never found its way into print. "The Frederick is great & fine, & happily situated; it is worthy of Berlin. But that other one. That other one is surely a blemish. That is, its most prominent & aggressive feature is. I refer to the golden angel on top of the Column of Victory . . . It is one of the unpleasantest angels that I have met. I believe I have not seen anything really unpleasanter in this line unless it may be some of those long slim pale anemic ones painted by Fra Angelo. But this is not that kind, but just the exact opposite. This is the Angel of Victory & is capable. I should like to see this one get after a flock of those others."

In this story, he also lauds another "monument," as he called it—a beggar. "It is the only beggar I have yet encountered in this vast city during my sojourn of three months & a half. I mean in public. The begging letter is in flourishing vogue here, & now & then you are visited by the beer-soaked humbug who has heard of something to his advantage in London or Vienna & must leave at once on the night train, & has called to borrow the needful money; but of the public beggar I have seen only that one sample. Necessarily he was conspicuous; necessarily he took hold of my retina & burnt his figure into it. He was wholly unexpected; he was a surprise, an electric shock, almost an incredibility. There he stood, backed up against a building in a lonely street, with a bare head, a bandaged eye, a wooden leg. His body bent forward, his seedy hat held out in his hand. Whenever in my mind's eye I see the Frederick & the Victory, I see also the wooden-legged beggar; unsummoned he drifts in & joins the couple & makes it a group. And he is not a smirch upon the group, but an honorable addition, because he stands for Law Enforced, not shirked. In all civilized cities there are carefully drawn & very stringent laws against public begging, but I did not suppose that there was a city where the police troubled themselves to carry them out."

Twain, however, was not as heartless as that might sound, since he did care whether the beggar, or poor people, for that matter, made a living. "Since Berlin enforces these laws against public begging. what measures does she take for the protection of the very poor & the friendless? It is a long story, but an interesting one I shall try to tell it some day & see if our people do not find in it things worth copying worth importing, for the sake of their good sense, their judiciousness & their large humanity." But sadly, the author never told that story, at least not in writing.

Maybe he was too busy with other issues. For instance, he and his friend Henry Fisher visited the Royal Library Unter den Linden, housed in a baroque building. The Juridical Faculty of Humboldt University is located today, and it is nicknamed *Kommode* (chest of drawers), for its shape. Twain noted that the library was fine, but it did not seem to have a printed catalogue. "You must know what you want before you get there," he remarked. "Some people keep Chinese & other books out many months, even years."

Fortunately, a librarian who recognized the famous writer showed Twain—and Fisher—around. Then he left them to their own devices amid a collection of antique letters. The letters were the private correspondence of the Prussian royals, mostly from and to Frederick the Great. They were in French, Frederick's favorite language. Fisher mentions a letter from the philosopher Francois Voltaire, addressed to the Prussian King, "but the poetry was too grossly indecent to have interest for persons outside of a psychopathic ward" (rather a lapse of judgment, one must say). Twain, in the meantime, found a handwritten manuscript of about ten pages, titled, *Tetragamy by Schopenhauer.*

The late philosopher Arthur Schopenhauer, a scholar of Immanuel Kant, was born in Danzig but had lived in Berlin for a couple of years. His main body of work, *The World as Will and Representation,* makes the point that human desires are futile, illogical, and troubling. Humankind, therefore, ought to adapt to an ascetic lifestyle—he sounded like an earthly version of Mr. Spock. Subsequently, he was never married, although he had a baby out of wedlock (who died at an early age), as well as a strained relationship with his mother. He believed that women were meant to obey (something his mother stubbornly refused to do), and that homo-

The former Royal Library, now a part of Humboldt University, today

sexuality thwarted at least the breeding of unworthy individuals, so it was not all bad (so he thought).

About Germans, Schopenhauer wrote, "For a German it is even good to have somewhat lengthy words in his mouth, for he thinks slowly, and they give him time to reflect." Maybe those sentences helped Twain relate to Schopenhauer; in any case, he picked up the pages, turned around, and asked Fisher what "tetragamy" meant. When the fellow correspondent explained that the term stood for having four wives, Twain joked, "Good! I have always wanted to reform monogamy, when my wife isn't looking." Then he asked Fisher to copy the pages (by hand), and translate them from their original German into English. Twain was not especially fond of Schopenhauer, though. He compared him to, as he called him, "queer Strindberg," who had only created female characters that were "hard-faced, sullen, cold-blooded, cheeky, grasping, vindictive, hell-raising, unvirtuous, unkind vixens." Anyone as misogynistic as those two, the author assumed, must be gay. In the end,

Danzig-born philosopher Schopenhauer lived in Berlin for several years.

he did not write about Schopenhauer. He did finish, however, his piece about the postal service, evidently drawing from his recent experiences on Körnerstrasse. He compared the postal service in Berlin to the post office in New York—not very flattering for the latter, but very much so for the former.

"The post offices [in Berlin] are certainly very plenty & scattered all over . . . The postal districts must count up very high as to number, for my latest address in Berlin (added in blue pencil at the post office) is 64 W. Indeed, those figures, with the word Berlin is a sufficient address. Letters frequently come which bear merely your name & the word Berlin; the post office does not add your street & its number, but only your postal district—as in this case, "64 W." The carrier soon finds you." Twain continued: "Even if you get lost yourself you are still safe, for the Department will find you. The name of a remote village, mis-spelt & illegibly written can baffle it for a while but not for long; the letter travels swiftly, here & there & everywhere, applying at all sorts of villages in all sorts of regions, till it hits the right place. There seems to be no red tape, no standing on quibbles, anywhere." He went on: "To get the work done. & done promptly & in the best manner is apparently the broad law of the Department. The perfection of the machine has been accounted for in this way. It is said that its great army of subordinates are educated young fellows who have been trained to the soldier's calling & are thus doubly equipped for their work: they are intelligent, instructed, & they are habituated to prompt obedience, hard work, &. diligent attention to duty. They start at the bottom . . . and climb thence by order of merit toward the top. Their places are not at the mercy of official caprice, they serve the country, not a party, & they are not required to help in politics."

Twain was even more impressed by the Rohrpost, a newly invented system of pneumatic tubes, about fifteen miles altogether, to transport letters within the city more quickly. Government offices and even hotels and warehouses had their own Rohrpost mailboxes. In 1876, the system opened to the public. "All Berlin is undermined; the tubes run everywhere. Your letter is shot through them like a telegram, & delivered at once," Twain wrote. "It is in a way the equivalent of our two-cent swift delivery; but it is much swifter & costs a little less." He also recalls a story about the Rohrpost that may or may not be true. "A physician who was suddenly called out of town on a Sunday morning dropped an ordinary penny postal card into a street box asking a young doctor to visit a patient for him at noon. But he got only the young doctor's name right, the rest of the address was some three miles out of the way. The postman found the indicated street & number, but necessarily not the doctor. But the post office hunted him out in the directory, posted 7 cents worth of stamps on the card, shot it through the pneumatic tube & delivered it on time. Although on weekdays, the postal deliveries seem to occur unceasingly, there is but one delivery on Sundays; & so, in addition to hunting out the doctor & contributing rohrpostage, the post office added a delivery not required on the Sabbath."

The tubes were heavily damaged in World War II, but the Rohrpost continued to operate. In 1963, two years after the Wall was built, the Rohrpost was closed to the public in West Berlin, and

During Twain's time in Berlin, the main post office, the Reichspostamt, *was situated at 16 Leipziger Strasse, at the corner of* Mauerstrasse. *It was built from 1871 to 1874 by architect Carl Schwatlo and was alreadye a post museum in 1897. Today, the Museum of Communication occupies the building. Up top is a sculpture of the globe, carried by giants, figurines from Greek mythology.*

closed to the city government in 1972. In East Berlin, the system was probably in use until the 1980s.

Twain also turned his attention to another new gimmick: The telegraph. "There are no telegraph poles, no telephone poles, no electric light poles in Berlin. These insane & exasperating & perilous objects are wholly absent. It seems to me that that is an idea worth copying. The electric light wires are under the ground, & the others are in the sky & out of the way. Here & there, on the top of a tall building one sees a huge iron cage like a bird cage; its wires are beaded all along with white spots—porcelain insulators; I have counted six hundred of them in one cage: from these insulators the wires radiate through the sky like vast rays of shadow, to various distant cages similarly perched." He gushed on—a message surely meant for the officials at home: "Telegraphing is very cheap & the service is so prompt & so excellent in every way that one doubts that this can be the same vehicle that is used by the Western Union gravel trains. The telephone service here is also excellent. I would like to compare it with ours, if we had one. But we have never had a telephone service which was entitled to anything but the compassion of the good & the blasphemies of the ungodly. It has always been deaf & dumb, when it wasn't dead—& it was usually that. At night, with the electric lights going, holding your ear to our telephone is as good as being in a battle, with an earthquake under foot & a thunderstorm overhead. Still, our telephone is a good property: any monopoly is a good property which collects money for a service & them shirks out of furnishing the service."

This was not the only Berlin invention Twain was fascinated with: In one of his letters, he mentioned the *Litfasssäule*, a free-standing cylindrical advertising column. The *Litfasssäule* made its inventor, printer, and publisher Ernst Litfass both wealthy and famous. The column was always surrounded by passers-by, informing them of the latest news, entertainment, theatres, and so on. It would be worth importing to the United States, Twain noted in his diary. "When Buffalo Bill was here, his biggest poster was probably not larger than the top of an ordinary trunk."

In the early days of January, Twain and Olivia traveled to Ilsenburg, near the Brocken in the Harz Mountains, the quintessential magical mountain of Germany—*Faust* includes a scene in which the witches are celebrating Walpurgis Night there. They roomed with Pastor Friedrich Wilhelm Orthmann, who ran a vacation rental business on the side. The Clemenses had gotten the address from Pastor John Henry Stuckenberg, the current—and first—pastor of the American Church in Berlin. They had dinner with some aristocrats of Ilsenburg, among them one very arrogant Count. The Count clearly felt that he was above mere mortals and refused to shake the hand of the local doctor's wife, something Twain found quite arrogant. Stuckenberg's successor, Dickie, however, complained to Twain later in New York that he had spoiled the Ilsenburg vacation for future Americans: after Twain had been there, Pastor Orthman raised the nightly rate from three to five marks.

When the couple returned to Berlin on January 12, 1892, Twain got more good news from Frederick Hall. Webster & Co. was ready to put out his recently finished book, *The American Claimant,* in the United States, while Chatto & Windus would publish it in England. Also, a new London magazine, *The Idler,* was planning to serialize it. In addition, Twain had managed to sell the German rights to a German publisher, *Deutsche Verlags-Anstalt*, based in Stuttgart (owned by Random House today). DVA was already in the process of translating it. Even though the book would not be such a great success in the long run, Twain could most certainly use the advance. Somewhat later, Hall told him that *Huckleberry Finn* had sold 17,000 copies in 1891, to Twain's great relief, since he would be getting royalties for that as well. The author closed this letter with "I've escaped the influenza so far." This, however, would prove to be premature.

One day later, Twain gave a lecture at the YMCA at 34 Wilhelmstrasse, at the invitation of Pastor Stuckenberg. On that occasion it was revealed that he did care for the church after all. The American church did not yet have a building of its own. However, the congregation planned to start construction on Motzstrasse, near Nollendorfplatz, and Twain supported the cause. His speech at the YMCA earned him 1257 marks and ninety pennies; and he donated the

A 1890s postcard from 34 Wilhelmstrasse, then the site of the YMCA. Today, the building is gone, and the lot is empty.

entire amount for the new building (the tycoon John D. Rockefeller would donate an even more substantial amount to the project).

The lecture was a great success, as the *Berliner Tageblatt* reported the next day. The *Tageblatt* had sent Gertraut Chales de Beaulieu, a travel writer and translator of English-language novels. She wrote under the name G. von Beaulieu, since women reporters at that time were quite uncommon and not widely accepted. The event felt like "Broadway in New York. American personalities, American conversations!" she gushed. The author managed to attract a huge, mainly American and English audience, among them many "pretty, young women with eccentric hats, with feathers bobbing and red ribbons." She described Twain as follows: "A pale, narrow, bold face under white, mane-like hair; small, dark, deep-set eyes twinkled under bushy, still-dark brows, then looked sharply observant into the distance; a curved nose with vaulted nostrils, a long, dark moustache over a quick-witted mouth and strong chin; atop a supple, nimble,

Wilhelmstrasse today has become a Disneyesque hot-spot for tourists looking for remnants of the Wall and Eastern Germany.

elegant figure." Beaulieu continued: "Mark Twain speaks dryly, seriously, supporting his speech with gestures, but never smiling, He read the "Tale of the Fishwife," and the story of the "Blue Jay" from his *A Tramp Abroad*. He also joked about one of the Berlin reporters' attempts to interview him. But, as he said, he so "utterly disappointed the man thirsting for knowledge that he—Mark Twain—was advised, for God's sake, to hermetically seal his mouth if he didn't want to thoroughly lose his reputation." Even more laughter shook the room when Twain addressed, once again, the German language. The reporter, however, would have been more interested in what the author thought about the city itself. "We've already read Hungarian, Italian, French, and Dutch descriptions of Berlin, but Mark Twain's accounts of Berlin customs, so far, have been lacking."

Twain made fun of his own German language skills as well. He once wrote in his diary that he was "complimented a good deal of my German in Berlin. On one occasion I emptied out a sentence of 47 words & it had only 63 grammatical errors in it." Somewhat later, he penned: "You have been a fool. If you had put in as many years improving your spiritual nature as you have put in on the G. language you could have been in heaven by this time." Henry Fisher even quipped that his colleague's German was getting worse over time instead of better. And the author himself believed that it was possible to learn English in thirty days and French in thirty weeks, whereas the German language required thirty years to learn properly. But Twain could actually speak German fairly well. He had started to learn the language at age fifteen, not all that uncommon then in the United States. Albert Locher documents an early letter by Twain, the application for his first visa in 1878, sent to then-Ambassador Bayard Taylor. Twain describes himself:

"Geborn 1835; 5 Fuss 8 ½ inches hoch; weight doch eher about 145 pfund, sometimes ein wenig unter, sometimes ein wenig oben; dunkel braun Haar und rhotes Moustache, full gesicht, mit sehr hohe Oren und leicht practvolles strahlenden Augen und ein Verdammtes gut moral character, Handlungkeit: Author von Bücher."

This is untranslatable, rather bad German, but Twain improved, as well as his wife and daughters. Grace King remarked in her book that the entire family spoke fluent German. When the family had traveled to Germany for the first time thirteen years earlier, Bigelow Paine noted that there was a "German nurse for the children, and the whole atmosphere of the household presently became lingually Teutonic."

Twain frequently contemplated in his diary how to utilize his German-lingo experiences in a book or a play. One such idea was a novel about a "hard-up American (who) takes classes in Berlin to teach English by Sauveur system [a method by Lambert Saveur, where only the teached language is spoken]. Knows not a word of German himself . . . Says he speaks G. as well as E., but has taken a pledge to never utter a word of it in his class. Has to be forever dodging encounters with his pupils on street, in church & everywhere (situation!)—pretty girl among pupils—beguiles him at last while he is bragging, to promise a G. speech somewhere—denouement." Sadly, this book remained unwritten, along with some other great ideas, such as a book about a "man who undertook to play deaf and dumb on a wager for 24 hours—first adventure occurs in a stage coach full of women."

But not every German was thrilled by Twain's rips on the German language. Albert Locher stumbled across a professor at Friedrich Wilhelm University, one H. Engel, who attended a lecture by Twain in the auditorium of a girls' school. "I was upset that a large part of the lecture was devoted to making fun of the German language," Engel wrote in a university magazine. "But most of the students and teachers present, who were teaching modern languages, did not seem to notice the lack of tact, because they were applauding wildly." Engel was also taken aback by Twain's southern drawl and his "sluggish walk," and he described the author like this: "A bushy moustache covered his lips for the most part; thick, bushy eyebrows cast a shadow over his large, expressive eyes, and his full white hair rose over a beautifully arched forehead." To make matters worse, the professor also had an acquaintance who had once shared a horse-drawn cab with Twain; the man was very disappointed that the author did not tell any jokes but complained about his rheumatism the whole time. It was an experience quite a few Berliners who met Twain had already made—or would make.

Twain had planned to return to Ilsenburg after the lecture, but a cold that progressed into pneumonia thwarted his plans. There was a stark temperature contrast between the warm YMCA and the ice-cold January air, and right after the speech, Twain and Olivia attended a ball at the von Versen's mansion and did not arrive back home until 2 a.m. In addition, the stoves in Ilsenburg had not been "satisfactory." The author had caught a heavy cold there already.

When Twain awoke the day after the lecture, he felt terrible. A doctor came to the Hotel Royal; the writer was diagnosed with congestion of the lungs and influenza and had to stay in bed for the next few weeks. His bedroom was unusually long and narrow, and he referred to it as the "sausage room," because it reminded him of a frankfurter. "If it had legs I would call it a dachshund," Twain said to Fisher, who paid a visit to his sick friend. Fisher tried to cheer Twain up. He brought him the Schopenhauer pages Twain had asked him

Wilhelmine of Preussen, Margravine and sister of Frederick the Great.

to copy from the Royal Library a few weeks earlier. But Olivia confiscated those papers, because she didn't want her husband to overtax himself with strenuous reading (or maybe Fisher had just claimed to have copied the pages, but had really been too lazy to do so). He also gave Twain a book the author had asked for, a memoir of Wilhelmine von Preussen, the sister and confidante of Frederick the Great. Wilhelmine later became the Margravine of Brandenburg-Bayreuth and founded the famous Bayreuth opera and theater.

Twain had been to Bayreuth twice, and the Margravine fascinated him so much that he even began to write a novel based on her life (he calls her Wilhelmina). He finished the first chapter—about her arrival in Bayreuth—as well as the notes for the second chapter. But he abandoned the manuscript, because his wife forbade him to work too much, and he never picked it up again. Only the fragments in this book remain, published here for the first time.

Fragment of Prussian History: Wilhelmina, Margravine of Bayreuth

By Mark Twain

It was mid-afternoon, January 22nd, 1732.

The day was dull & cold & lowering. The land was veiled in a leaden mist. There was snow on the ground; it had thawed to a mushy slush, but was beginning to freeze, now, as the short day closed down. One could see but a mile or two ahead, because of the mist, & the aspects revealed were dreary & depressing. The land lay in rugged swales & billows; there was a lonesome tree here & there, looming dim in the mist, but mainly the landscape was naked, void of moving life, & desolate.

Across it a train of carriages & wagons was laboring. Not comfortably; but heaving, swaying, creaking & crunching along through the deep ruts & mid-boles at a snail's pace. The train consisted of five lumbering carriages of a pretentious sort, drawn by lean & scraggly post-horses; & seven heavily-freighted baggage vans drawn by farmstead pick-ups.

The first coach had six horses. On the box with its driver sat two drowsing men-servants, well muffed up, & in the rear boot stood a couple of guards with ancient firelocks. On the roof were two large trunks, which were not very securely fastened, & these traveled around here & there with the lurchings of the coach, with the air of creatures interested in the scenery & anxious to look over the side as often as possible. Bunched up on the forward seat within, sat a stalwart young man steeped in a deep sleep. This was Prince Henry, heir to the crown & sceptre of the Margraveship of Bayreuth. He was a good young fellow, but commonplace.

In the back seat sat his small bride of twenty-two, Wilhelmina, Margravine to-be, & eventual celebrity. Because of her voluminous wraps, nothing was visible of her but her face. But it was a striking one. For it was alive & alert with bright intelligence. In that dull age & society this made it not merely striking but astonishing. This vivid countenance was a window which was not usually curtained; oftener than was wise, & oftener than was intended, it betrayed to the outsider a view of what was going on within. This was not fortunate, in a day when most suits of clothes contained a combination of spy, hypocrite & traitor.

The nature, character & disposition revealed by the face had some features which were very good indeed, & some which were not so good. The girl's bent was toward kindliness, she was sympathetic, her feelings were intense, she was uncommonly loyal, both to her likes & her dislikes. She had come up in a bitter hard school, yet she was not morose nor soured, but kept the fires of a naturally sunny spirit burning pretty steadily in spite of unpropitious conditions; she had had no rational training, yet often, in trying circumstances she exhibited a patience which was wisdom, & at rarer intervals charted out an active diplomatic course for herself which did not go wholly to ruin. She was proud of her royal origin; also, she was longingly ambitious. But her quality of qualities was one which set her in the midst of a horizonless solitude in Germany—humor. She had a flaming abundance of it, but it was a sun in an empty sky; there was no fellowship for it. Sometimes she made it convey warmth & cheer & pleasure & refreshment, but mainly she burnt people with it. Judged by the standards of her time she was refined & delicate in feeling & expression; judged by our standards she was not. In education, character, disposition, behavior, morals, intellect, intention, & the faculty of expression with tongue & pen, she was well above the best competitor in the little society at whose social & political summit—barring a step—she was now about to take her place.

Beside the young thing sat a motherly good-hearted, thick-headed, eager, interested, affectionate, anxious, half-wise, indiscreet, over-zealous, garrulous, middle-aged noblewoman—Chief Maid of Honor to the girl, & furnished to her along with her husband & the rest of her variegated outfit by papa & mama, King & Queen of Prussia.

The second coach was filled with minor maids of honor belonging to the young girl's train.

In the third coach was the Baron von Reitzenstein, Grand Chamberlain of the Bayreuth Court; also the Baron von Burstell, Prussian Envoy Extraordinary & Minister Plenipotentiary, newly appointed by the King to represent him at Bayreuth, & at the same time keep an eye upon his daughter's interests; also several high officials of the young princess's household—selected for her by papa & mamma.

The two other coaches were stocked with household servants of minor degree.

The six baggage wagons brought up the rear.

A few flakes of snow made their appearance & went slanting by on the wind. The princess noticed them & said—

"I will not go on with my dream at this time; it is not suited to the weather & the general aspects."

The elder lady's bored face brightened eagerly.

"I've been dying with the silence, your Royal Highness, & praying the dear God to move you to break it! Is it proper to ask what the dream is about?"

"Oh, nothing. Nothing but the four royal crowns promised me in the cradle. Four phantoms. It's all they are. I shan't ever see them, and it vexes me to think of it!"

"Oh, pray don't talk so, madam! I can't bear to hear you. I have always believed in that beautiful prophecy."

"And so have I. Oh, yes, & it has vexed me & pestered

me ever since I could walk; for it never comes true, but always keeps putting itself off—& off—& off."

"Why, madam, you forget. You came very near being the future queen of England."

"*Near* it! What does that prove? It didn't happen. It failed. It was a bitter disappointment—just as bitter as it could be. And it could have been managed, too, & through foolishness & blundering, it wasn't. I cried my eyes out about it. Anybody would! England-ah, just think what a throne that is—& what glories shine upon it out of its imposing old history!"

"Ah, but madam! It is matter for patience; only just patience & courage, that is all. It is going to come right, I know it. Everything that was foretold by that sorcerer came true—ah, he was the wonder of the world, that man, I remember him well!—& this will come true, too. Yes, you will see. And besides, you must remember, madam, if your poor servant may make bold to say such a thing, that you are only a child, yet. Indeed there is plenty of time, & it will all happen."

"How, plenty of time, you good, credulous, thoughtless old thing? I am twenty-two. & the fulfilment not yet begun, look at the average! At this rate I should be eighty-eight when I got the fourth. I should be a shriveled-up mummy, & I wouldn't want it & wouldn't have it!"

"Ah, but dear lady, the fulfilment is really on its way—one cannot deny that. The royal crown of Bayreut[h] is destined to rest upon your head, & here sleeps he that will place it there. The other three will follow."

The young princess glanced at the sleeper, & her irritated face softened & the light of love shone in her eyes. She bent over & snuggled the wraps about him deftly & gave them a love-pat. The Chief Maid of Honor searched the landscape with a longing eye, then said, sorrowfully—

"It will never, never come to an end—this journey. Eleven days of slop & sludge & ice & snow, & rain & sleet, & desert & desolation, & weary drag, drag, *drag*! the longest two hundred miles that ever was, & your Royal Highness out of health & no more fit for it than—dear me, I do believe I see Bayreuth! I am sure there is a little town away off yonder under the horizon. Look, madam!"

"Yes, it does seem to be a town. And of course it is our royal capital. And think—it could have been London—*would* have been London, but for that stupid blundering! Or Dover—or Plymouth. And then—why then, covering all the sea there would be fleets of battle-ships, clothed in fluttering flags from mast-head to water-line, & filling the world with smoke & the thunder of cannon; & onshore a gorgeous reception-pavilion, & there a crowd of gorgeous princes & dukes & admirals & generals, waiting, & beyond them a vista of triumphal arches, & multitudes of people in holiday clothes waving hats and handkerchiefs, & a whole great army of troops—oh, regiment after regiment—cavalry, artillery, infantry, in handsome uniforms, & the Troops of the Guard!—think of the Troops of the Guard, horsed like kings, & blazing like the sun in their brazen breastplates and helmets—"

Pop! Pop! Pop!

"What was that—a dog?"

"No, your Royal Highness, it was cannon. A salute. Here is the Escort. And with it the Royal Court. They are coming into view, now, as we turn around this little hill."

The princess took a quick glimpse, & said, with dismay—

"What, these sorry savages, this fantastic tagrag & bobtail?"

She touched her husband to rouse him, then drew herself up in state, for Herr von Dobenek, Governor of Bayreuth, with his aid[e]s, was approaching, to read his Address of Welcome. The princess muttered—

"Museum of antiquities. These clothes are historical relics; no, they go back further than that. Even the very ribbons on the pigtails are dim with age."

She slightly inclined her head in recognition of the Governor's profound bow, & the reading of the address was begun. It was pretty windy, & pretty ornate, & pretty long, & came near being tedious; but the Governor's pride in it, his joy in its rolling periods, & the energy of his gesticulations & the crash & thunder of his extraordinary delivery saved it from that. The princess answered with a proper word or two, the escort moved to its place in the van, & the procession took up its march.

It marched to the scream & clatter & bow-wow of six fifes, six kettle-drums and three hundred pleased & astonished dogs, & plowed its slow way between a double pile of wooden-shod peasants, who uncovered reverently & kept up such a sincere & noisy welcome as the princess passed along that she was touched—touched almost to the verge of happiness. Almost. She could not be quite happy. She had had too rude a surprise, too grotesque an awakening from her gilded dream, too sharp a disappointment. The unromantic picture of the Court kept rising before here, those thirty frowsy nobles in the seedy clothes. "Hostlers," she called them, to herself, & afterwards described their faces in her private diary, & said they were of a sort to scare children to bed with. And that was not all, nor the most delicately worded, that she said about them; for although in spiritual charity & in refinement of feeling she was a century & a half in advance of her time, there was in her something of the plain-speaking taint of her day, & she often allowed it to take the air. Her speeches were not often really coarse, but with a most generous frequency they were vitriolic. Other people said brutal things in a brutal way; she said hard things, but not brutally; she phrased them sharply, delivered them cheerily & good-humoredly, & yet where they struck they were likely to take off a bit of the hide.

As the procession dragged along, that golden feature, that saving feature of her makeup-humor-came to her relief, as it was to do in a thousand troubled days of her after life, & her spirits revived. The humor of the situation gradually forced itself upon her, & humor's healthy handmaid, wisdom, followed, with the advice that the most profitable thing to do with any condition of things, however disappointing, is to cheer up & make the best of it. The princess resolved to at least try to be cheerful, & to compel success eventually if she could; & she hoped that circumstances would help, though at bottom she felt dubious about that.

At the end of half an hour the procession came tooting and drumming into the shabby little town, & went winding about through narrow streets that were blocked with huzzaing villagers & decorated with flapping & fluttering rags & flags, & a little before nightfall it arrived before the Castle of the monarch.

Pop! pop! pop! went the little cannon-salute again, the fifes screamed, the drums rumbled, the assembled citizenship cheered, & the three hundred country dogs & the two hundred village dogs opened their jaws & raised the volume of welcoming noise away above royal degree & made it imperial. Later, Wilhelmina wrote in her journal, "*Ich glaube nicht, dass je eine Fürstin so empfangen wurde.*" Freely translated: I doubt if any princess ever got just such a reception before.

The Castle was not a castle; still it was usual to call the residence of a German monarch by that title, just as the residence of a Bishop has to be called a palace, even when it is only a South Sea island wigwam. There was nothing large about the Margrave's castle except its name. It was a dull-colored stone house as square as a box, & had not ornamentation of any sort about it. It stood in the midst of a great, dismal, walled court-yard which was roughly paved with stone. A pair of sentries in faded uniform stood guard at the gate, & a duplicate pair guarded the door.

The prince & the princess descended, walked on a red carpet to the door, the sentries presenting arms in due form, & entered. In the hall stood the monarch with his two young-lady daughters, in the subdued light of a cautious economy of candles, & their state was supported by the thirty nobles whom we have already met. They probably got in the back way.

The Margrave received the pair with a grandeur of style & an elaboration of solemn graces & posturings which made him a fair-to-good imitation of the model which he was without doubt trying to copy—the late Louis XIV. The imitation extended further—& successfully; for the Margrave had a little body & spindle legs, & upon the first hung the wide-skirted gold-laced coat of Louis' time—satin, new & glistering—& the legs were in the grip of silk stockings that came to the knee & were gartered there. The small head was lost in a wig which was a Niagara of tumbling curls—a fashion which commoner people were forsaking for the less showy tie-wig. Court sword, lace cuffs, gold snuff-box, smile graduated to the rank of the person to beatified by it—it was all there, & the valuable part of Louis still survived, though the rest of him was gone out of the world. The Margrave said many fine and gracious things to his new daughter & to his son, & went through his whole act without missing a word or making a flaw. For it was his best suit that he had on, & he was feeling good. And besides, he was sober, this time. All noticed it, & all admired it.

He was forty-five years old, he was a Royal Personage; he had over 43,000 subjects; in his capital dwelt upwards of 2,000 people, & he was master of a realm which it would take a pigeon more than half an hour to fly across. "Dominions," he called it. He was what he was, not by appointment of man but by the grace of God. These mistakes were always being made in those days.

The Margrave & his daughters took the travel-worn little princess up stairs at once to show her her quarters, & the whole aristocratic menagerie followed. First, there was a large hall, which was pretty dirty. It opened into her room of state, which was large & lofty, but had probably not been whitewashed for ages. The carpet had been pretty once; the furniture had been trustworthy in some former time, but it needed shoring up, now. The walls were hung with tapestries which had once contained Moses & Aaron & the children of Israel in the wilderness, but they had all got away now but the wilderness. At least nothing was left but faint, uncertain ghosts of the wanderers, life-size phantoms, filmy, wavering, vanishing forms flitting across the once Red Sea, appealing to the obliterated uplifted serpent, worshiping the place where the golden calf had been in brighter days; & in the funereal shed by the candles this uncanny show made the princess's flesh creep. She said that the faded face eyed her like spectres.

This salon opened into a cabinet which was hung with brocade of a color no longer determinable. Next was a room whose bewitched & bedeviled extravagances of poverty & ruin not even her irreverent pen was able to descriptively damn to her satisfaction. Here, as previously in the salon & the cabinet, she kept a determined grip on her wayward tongue, & to all the Margrave's complacent inquiries after her opinion answered with a reluctant but courteous "*Schön—wunderschön!*—Beautiful—wonderfull beautiful!"

And finally, her bedroom. It was upholstered in formerly green damask with gold trimmings; all the belongings of the place decrepit with age & service, about down with this life, & ready for the last consolations of the church. Every time anyone touched the bed curtains a rag fell away.

"How does it please you?" said his Royal Highness.

"*Schön-wunderschön*," sighed the exile.

On January 24—after being bedridden for eleven days—Twain finally got a break: His cousin Alice von Versen came to visit, and she invited him to the imperial palace to "witness the consecration of some flags." But Twain was forced to turn down the invitation. She came back the next day, however, and told him that Kaiser Wilhelm II had commanded her to "prepare dinner for him & me in her house," as soon as Twain was well enough. The Kaiser believed that a dinner at a private residence would not put such a strain on the ailing author.

Twain's recovery would take quite some time, though, during which he celebrated his twenty-second wedding anniversary, but mostly just looked out of the "sick-room window," at Pariser Platz and Unter den Linden. He observed horses, dogs, busses, policemen, and traffic in general, which he deemed fast ("nothing like it but in London"), and he took notes. "All the swell carriages are out," he wrote February 10, when two royal carriages had passed through the "middle compartment of the Brandenburger Thor." The folks on the street took their hats off, but the "Emperor's carriages & liveries are much less showy than many of the nobility's." Shortly thereafter, he saw the King and the Queen of Württemberg at the Brandenburg Gate. "They double-banked the Holy Land with soldiers—who shouted 'He's coming.'" Twain added, "I would like to be the Emperor for a while."

Twain became bored. Soon he complained that he was tired of staying in bed—especially after the rheumatism also crept into his right foot—and he mocked the quality of European coffee in his diary, which he deemed "worthless." He also asked Olivia to get him wine jelly, American crackers, and baked American apples. On February 14, Professor von Helmholtz called. Telephones were still rare then, but fancy hotels had them.

Twain now had the time to read a lot of books and newspapers, "in a state of excited ignorance," and he came to the conclusion that "The 'Court Gazette' of a German paper can be covered with a playing card. In an English paper the movements of titled people take up about three times that room. In the papers of Republican France, from six to sixteen times as much." He also noted that German papers were tasteless, slovenly, and ugly—even "worse than the French," whereas papers in London or New York were "clean and beautiful."

The papers also helped him to keep up with current politics. He became interested in a debate in the Reichstag about the *Öffentliches Militärgericht* (public military trial), which he called a "circus." It was about whether military tribunals should be held publicly, but he never managed to understand it fully. "I read all the debates on that question with a never-fading interest but all at once they spring a vote on me a couple of days ago & and did *something* by vote of 100 to 143, but I could not find out what it was." He moved on to the *Schulgesetzentwurf* (draft for a school bill), writing in his diary, "Don't know what a *Schulgesetzentwurf* is, but I keep as excited over it and as worried about it as if it were my own child. I *simply* live on the Sch-E; it is my daily bread. I wouldn't have the question *settled* for anything in the world."

Twain probably knew very well what he was talking about. Not only did Jean frequent a public school in Berlin, he was also acquainted with the Deputy Secretary of the Interior, Karl Heinrich von Boetticher, who was involved with the bill. The *Schulgesetzentwurf* would give organized religion, mainly the Catholic Church, authority over the curriculum of elementary schools. The bill was a concession that the Kaiser and his Prime Minister, Leo von Caprivi, were prepared to make to placate the Catholic Center Party and the Conservative Party in the Reichstag. It backfired, though, because the Liberal Party protested against the law, which it deemed too church-friendly. And Twain definitely did not like it either, because he was a church-skeptic, if not an outright atheist. While musing about the *Schulgesetzentwurf,* he noted that Germany "recognized 2 sects, Catholic & Lutheran; (which appear to differ from each other nearly as much as a red-headed man differs from an auburn-headed man). These receive State support & their schools receive State support. Other sects are taxed to support these sects & schools & have to run their own churches & schools at their own costs. It is infamous." Twain was also not impressed by Caprivi in general (whom the Kaiser would fire two years later). He once noted that the Chancellor "seems angry when talks loud—different with me." Twain

The Kaiser is riding along Unter den Linden to the Brandenburg Gate....

took note of another occurrence, the trial against *Kladderadatsch*, a satirical Berlin weekly paper (the title loosely translates as "loud noisemaker"), founded in 1848 by David Kalisch, a liberal German Jewish comedian and playwright. The magazine was famous for its caricatures of Prussian politicians. In 1891, the paper was sued for defamation, because it had called the Holy Coat of Treves—a robe that was supposedly worn by Jesus before he was crucified—a fraud. The robe is retained in the Cathedral of Trier, a German city founded by the Romans. But *Kladderadatsch* was acquitted, to Twain's relief. "As if there were any 'real relicts'—or ever had been," he wrote.

Twain also kept plotting his aforementioned book, *Recent European Glimpses* (he had not come up with a better title yet). He asked Frederick Hall to hold back for now, but he promised to deliver the manuscript by the next summer, presumably 1893. He wanted to collect the six European travel letters commissioned by McClure, but he was not satisfied with them yet. "Of the five already published I like

.... while the bed-ridden author one floor above is taking notes.

only three—& not all of the three," he wrote to his British publisher, Chatto & Windus. He also planned to add a lot more chapters to the book. However, *Recent European Glimpses* would never materialize; nor would a book on Berlin, despite all of those Berliners, beginning with reporter Max Horwitz, who had asked for one.

    Finally, after thirty days of illness, Twain was allowed to get up to meet the Emperor at the von Versen's place at 36 Mauerstrasse, around the corner from the Hotel Royal. It was February 20, 1892, only about two weeks before the family was due to leave Berlin. Twain had penned his thoughts about the encounter beforehand: "In that day the imperial lion and the democratic lamb shall sit together, and a little General shall feed them" (the little general to which he referred was Maximilian von Versen, who was rather short and small of stature). The invitation came on an "engraved card as big as an atlas," and it threw Twain into a frenzy, because it required "Frock coat—black cravat," meaning black tie and evening attire.

His young daughter, Jean, who adored the Kaiser, was even more impressed. "I wish I could be in papa's clothes," she said after hearing about the invitation, and added after some consideration, "But that wouldn't be any use. I reckon the Emperor wouldn't recognize me." Later, she told him, "Papa, the way things are going, pretty soon there won't be anybody left for you to get acquainted with but God." (Twain attributes the same quote to Jean, however, after they both met Poultney Bigelow in November.)

The evening before the dinner, Twain was briefed by Rudolf Lindau, who advised him to pay attention with whom the Emperor talked, and for how long—this would be a good way to judge the guests' standing. "In Berlin, as in the imperial days of Rome, the Emperor was the sun." Lindau explained. The Emperor would move from group to group, and any small-talk lasting longer than four minutes meant that the guest was in very good graces. This "imperial thermometer" was important for Lindau. He was in the service for thirty years and hadn't had a vacation longer than a fortnight (as Twain told Paine). So "he was weary all through, to the bones and the marrow now, and was yearning for a holiday of a whole three months." Such a request was not possible; an official was supposed to tender his resignation and settle for a sabbatical.

Lindau was sure Leo von Caprivi would go along, but it was the emperor who called the shots, and not the chancellor. During the evening, the emperor talked to pretty much everybody for less than four minutes—the last man he turned to was Lindau. He put his hand on Lindau's shoulder and talked to him for seven minutes straight; so Lindau asked for a full six months off—and got it. He was even given a diplomatic post in Constantinople—known as Istanbul today—where he had nothing to do except "attend banquets of an extraordinary character at the embassy once or twice a year," Twain wrote.

Lindau and Twain were not the only guests at the von Versens'. The Kaiser's brother, Prince Heinrich—or Henry, as the Americans called him—was present, along with Prince Hugo von Radolin, a high-ranking diplomat of Polish heritage in the Kaiser's court, and some more royals and officers, including Twain's acquaintance Fritz von Rottenburg from the German Foreign Service. All told, there were fourteen guests at the table.

The Kaiser not only spoke English fluently, "flawlessly," as Twain pointed out—after all, he was the grandson of Queen Victoria of England (as a five-year-old, he reportedly greated her once with: "Hello, old duck.") And he was also a big fan of Twain's work. He especially liked his story on Heidelberg in *A Tramp Abroad*, along with his book, *Old Times on the Mississippi*. Twain found the encounter interesting, though he was not accustomed to not being the center of a conversation, but instead had to listen to the Kaiser for most of the time. In fact, he had cautioned himself beforehand that the "Emperor was host, therefore, according to my own rule, he had a right to do the talking, and it was my honorable duty to intrude no interruptions or other improvements except upon invitation." And so he did.

Twain had the distinct feeling that the night had ended on a sour note, however, though he did not quite know why. The explanation he came up with in his later memoires was this: The Kaiser had praised the U.S. military's veteran pension system, but Twain had quite a different opinion. "In the beginning our government's generosity to the soldier was clean in its intent, and praiseworthy, since the pensions were conferred upon soldiers who had earned them, soldiers who had been disabled in the war and could no longer earn a livelihood for themselves and their families," Twain pointed out. But that eventually changed. "The pensions decreed and added later lacked the virtue of a clean motive, and had little by little degenerated into a wider and wider and more and more offensive system of vote-purchasing, and had now become a source of corruption, which was an unpleasant thing to contemplate, and was a danger besides."

The emperor was quite monosyllabic toward the author, after the latter had expressed that thought. "I quite clearly remember the effect which my act produced—to wit, the Emperor refrained from addressing any remarks to me afterward, and not merely during the brief remainder of the dinner, but afterwards," Twain noticed. After dinner, the whole party moved to the smoking room in the basement of the von Versen home, where "cigars, beer, and anecdotes would be in brisk service until midnight." The place, called "the tunnel," was decorated "after the style of the ancient Potsdam." At midnight, the emperor shook hands and left. "I am sure that the Emperor's good night was the only thing he said to me in all that time," Twain recalls in his memoires.

Since Twain was invited in the following weeks by two Prussian princesses for breakfast, he had probably not behaved so badly after all. And Kaiser Wilhelm himself had a different recollection of that night—he complained that the author had been *too* quiet. Wilhelm II would write in his own memoires later that Twain was a prime example of a humorist who happened to be quite listless in person, and who did not act the same way his literary character did. Again, a common complaint about Twain. But if the Kaiser did indeed believe that Twain was boring, it was a misconception. Not only had Twain tried to be subdued, he was generally poignant and satirical, but he did not like comic exaggeration. He was far from a clown who felt the constant need to tell jokes, as other Berliners had learned before. Twain never published anything about his encounter with the Kaiser, and these notes were only allowed to be made public after his death, in accordance with his own decree.

Twain would see the Kaiser again, but only from afar, from his hotel room. Germany's unprecedented economic boom lasted until 1914. But amid the financial success, there was also a stark contrast of immense poverty. The trade paper *Berliner Börsen-Zeitung* stated in November 1891, that more than 22,000 homeless people inhabited Berlin. These poor folks couldn't even afford the cheap backyard tenements. The number of unemployed workers would eventually rise to 70,000. In addition, there was also growing dissatisfaction especially among Liberals and Social Democrats with the Kaiser and von Caprivi, who were accused of being too conservative, and their infamous *Schulgesetz*, which Twain had made fun of, was seen as the ultimate proof. On top of that, the Kaiser had emphasized in a speech on February 24, 1892, that everybody who was dissatisfied with the government should "shake the German sand out of their slippers & leave."

This was the final insult to tick off the already disgruntled Berliners. The day after this speech, tens of thousands of people, many of them poor, but quite a few of them outraged Liberals and Social Democrats, got together for a rally on Unter den Linden. The rally marched all the way up to the city castle, to the Kaiser, passing the Hotel Royal. "The speech had made a great stir," Twain wrote in his diary. "That & the odious (proposed) Schulgesetz & the lack of bread & work resulted in a mob gathering in front of the palace yesterday, of people out of work. They uttered revolutionary cries. Bakery bread was distributed to them, but they threw it away." The rally continued for days. "Crowds of the proletariat drift up and down the Holy Land today. But the Emperor rode out as usual, & after him I saw the whole force of royal carriages following—apparently all the royal women & all the children have turned out to show that they are not afraid."

Jean also watched the rally. "For a few days there was quite an unruly mob here, which went crying for bread through the streets, and when it was given to them they threw it around the street," she noted in her diary. "They threw a policeman off his horse. The soldiers and police were a little too much for them." At Jean's school, the children were forbidden to speak about the uprising, as Twain noted as well, "but they said they'd tell her out of school."

Two days later, Twain attended a society dinner at the house of Secretary Coleman, from the American embassy, where Rottenburg was present, along with the von Versens and Adolf Wermuth. Wermuth, who would later become mayor of Berlin, was the commissioner the German government would send to the Chicago World's Fair of 1893 (there, Wermuth became the regular companion of Bertha Palmer, the wife of Potter Palmer, the richest man in Chicago). The ties between Berlin and Chicago were close; for instance, a Berlin delegation had visited Chicago to study the slaughterhouses, since Berlin planned to expand its slaughterhouses in the borough known today as Prenzlauer Berg. Twain noted that this time he was wearing a black tie, while everyone else was wearing a white one ("Just my luck"). But he did not mention the rally at the dinner, or in any of his writings, except briefly in his diary. Maybe he just didn't think it was important, or he was too impressed by the Kaiser.

The Berlin city castle on the Spree, at the end of Unter den Linden. It was destroyed in World War II, the ruins were torn down by the GDR.

But there was another famous witness of the uprising: Heinrich Mann, the brother of Nobel laureate Thomas Mann. Heinrich Mann, then a student at the Friedrich Wilhelm University, became famous for *The Blue Angel,* the book on which Marlene Dietrich's first movie was based. Mann depicted the uprising in his landmark novel, *The Loyal Subject,* seen through the eyes of bourgeois underling Diederich Hessling. "In those wet and cold days of February 1892, Diederich spent a lot of time on the street," Mann wrote. He noticed that something was happening on Unter den Linden. "The jobless!" They came from the north, in small groups, slow, standing everywhere. "A policeman on a horse, yelling, urged them to keep moving, to the next corner"—where they stood again, wide, hollow faces, in front of the strong walls of the castle. More and more of the jobless congregated along Unter den Linden, gathering, running, and closing in on the castle, "like water breaking through the levees." They carried banners, "Bread!

The ruins of the castle today. The cellars have been excavated, since the castle is being rebuild. The gate in the background is the last remainder.

Work!" And they were also crying for bread and work, words "surging over the masses like a thundercloud; bread! Work!"

"But the mounted police attacked the crowd, using batons. The crowd did not yield, however. They rose up, and—female voices in the mix—kept yelling, 'Bread! Work!'" A couple of men broke the windows of a fancy café on Unter den Linden, which filled up quickly with poor people. Tables were knocked over. Suddenly someone yelled. "Isn't that Wilhelm!" In fact, the Kaiser had left the castle, on horseback, to show himself, to calm the rebellious folks down. The bourgeois bystanders, Diederich among them, were relieved, since they sided with the Kaiser. "Kids, this is a historical moment," one of Diederich's acquaintances said. And while the Kaiser's loyal subjects waved at him, and shouted, and hailed him, Wilhelm rode his horse through the Brandenburg Gate, leaving the poor and the jobless behind.

In March 1892, Twain and Olivia left Berlin, at the advice of their doctors, with Susy and Jean in tow. They headed to a warmer climate in the south of France, to the city of Menton, and later to Vienna. Only Clara remained in Berlin, to continue her study of music. It was astonishing that her father permitted this, considering the arguments they had over Clara's fondness of dashing young officers (and vice versa).

Twain returned to Berlin on June 28, but for only a few days. He was picked up at the train station by Clara, Mary Willard, his daughter's music teacher, and Secretary Jackson from the embassy, with whom he stayed. He took the opportunity to meet all of his friends and acquaintances. The next day, he had breakfast with Marian Phelps, and lunch with Clara at Ms. Willard's place. Later, he stopped by at the American embassy at the Kaiserhof and got together with Secretary Coleman. In the evening, he paid a visit to the von Versens on Mauerstrasse, left a card for the British ambassador, and ended the night with Jackson. He also promised pretty much everybody, including Phelps, Lindau, and even Mommsen, a copy of his semi-pornographic book, *1601*, which takes place in Tudor England and was published under a pseudonym, but he probably never followed through. "Berlin *is* a wonderfully fine city & its government is a model," was one of his last notes about the city. And he even made peace with the golden angel. "The 'Victory' statue is wretched only from behind," he noted.

Twain returned to Berlin a second time, for a lecture during the summer of 1893. A few months later, he met a Hohenzollern Princess in Vienna, presumably Charlotte of Preussen, the younger sister of Wilhelm II, who had been a socialite in Berlin before she married Bernhard, the Count of Sachsen–Meiningen. She told Twain that Maximilian von Versen had died, and that she knew about his dinner with the emperor in the von Versens' home. While they were talking, the Princess was taking such a zealous anti-clerical stance that Twain scolded her that "*she* shouldn't have such opinions as that—they were properer to my sort of folk." At the time, Twain was working on a book on Joan of Arc, the medieval French revolutionary who was burned at the stake on behalf of the Church

Twain's Berlin is commemorated throughout the city: the Rudolf Virchow hospital, Mommsen Street, Bismarck Street, which is also a busy subway station, the elevated train station Mendelssohn-Bartholdy-Park, a pharmacy at Helmholtzplatz, and Schopenhauer Street (in Potsdam).

of England. The Princess requested that he send her a copy as soon as the book was printed, which he did.

But Joan of Arc could not prevent Twain's ever-looming bankruptcy. The following year, at sixty, he lost everything. And he wouldn't write any more great novels, either. *Pudd'nhead Wilson*—an account of racism in America—was his last work of fiction. Desperately needing money, he went on a tour around the world that netted him about $200,000, so he could pay off his debts in full. The tour also supplied him with material for a lecture series, articles, and a new travel book, *Following the Equator*. He was accompanied by Clara and Livy. But they paid a hefty price: They were not present when beloved Susy died of meningitis.

Olivia would never really recover from that tragedy. She died in 1904 in Florence, Italy. Twain had her gravestone at the family plot in Elmira, New York, engraved in German, the language he'd grappled with his whole life. *Gott sei dir gnädig, O meine Wonne!* (God be merciful unto you, Oh my Joy!). "Why can't I go with her," the mourning husband wrote to a friend.

A few years later, Jean lost her life due to an epileptic seizure. Only Clara, Twain's last surviving child, had success in life as an opera singer. She married not a dashing young officer, but a renowned pianist, Ossip Gabrilowitsch. They had met in Vienna in 1899, where the family lived; both were studying music (Rudolf Lindau, who had retired by then, paid a visit to Twain in Vienna, too). Later, Clara spent a concert season with her husband in Berlin. "They have taken a house in Berlin," Twain told *The New York Times* in 1909—presumably not on Körnerstrasse. Clara also had a reconciliatory reunion with her former Berlin piano teacher, Moritz Moszkowski. When Moszkowski died penniless in Paris, Gabrilowitsch organized a benefit concert for his funeral.

Berlin would stay in the author's heart. He kept in touch with Lindau via mail, who had moved to Helgoland after he retired—in a letter from 1902, Twain wished Helgoland was in Upstate New York, where the family was settled at the time. That same year, he was once again reminded of his Berlin adventures, when he met the emperor's brother, Prince Henry, at a banquet in Manhattan. According to Bigelow Paine, the banquet was held by the mayor of New York City. Twain wrote in his notes, however, that it was given by Herman Ridder, the publisher of the *Staats-Zeitung*, then one of the biggest German-language papers in America. According to Vic Fischer from the Mark Twain Library, there were two dinners in February, which Prince Henry attended, so both were possible. Twain was not invited to speak on that occasion (which was quite unusual), and the author assumed that the prince was still sulking over that "breach of etiquette" in Berlin, and had "crisscrossed his name with a pencil." The prince did talk with him, however, "cordially and humanly attentive during a considerable portion of the evening," as Twain noted himself, so maybe it had just been a coincidence.

Five years later, Twain met an American official in New York City, who had been part of a delegation to Berlin to negotiate a long-disputed tariff treaty with the Kaiser. He brought Twain a message from Wilhelm II: "Convey to Mr. Clemens my kindest regards. Ask him if he remembers that dinner, and ask him why he didn't do any talking." Twain lamented, "Why, how could I talk when he was talking! He held the ace, as the poker-clergy say, and two can't talk at the same time with good effect.... If I were not too old to travel, I would go to Berlin.... I would say, 'Invite me again, Your Majesty, and give me a chance'; then I would waive rank and do all the talking myself."

Twain also was still interested in German politics. On April 8, 1907, Herman Ridder gave a dinner for Charlemagne Tower, the American Ambassador to Germany, at the Manhattan Club in Madison Square Park, to celebrate some initial progress of said tariff negotiations. Twain was present, along with German-American luminaries such as Carl Schurz, Jakob Schiff, Peter Cooper Hewitt, and Ralf Pulitzer. In a letter two days later, Twain congratulated "Dear Excellenz"—presumably Tower—on his "most admirable speech," and mentioned a "young gentleman," Robert Haven Schauffler. "He will explain to you his 'Century'-mission to the *Vaterland*—a matter which promises to be of interest & value to both Germany & America," Twain promised. Schauffler, who had studied in Berlin, wrote for the *Century* literary magazine, and

Miriam von Versen in her gallery Froschhammer & Rosenvogel *at Auguststrasse. This part of town has been revived since the Wall fell.*

became a famed poet and musician. But whatever his mission was, it never came up again. For unknown reasons, the letter ended up with Lindau.

Twain's last wish was granted on April 21, 1910. When he left this world, Halley's Comet appeared in the sky, just as it had shown up seventy-five years earlier, when he was born.

Very little remains of Mark Twain's Berlin today. Not only is the house at 7 Körnerstrasse gone; but the Hotel Royal, the Hotel Bristol, the Kaiserhof, the English House on Mohrenstrasse, the YMCA on Wilhelmstrasse, the Hotel de Rome, the von Versens' residence on Mauerstrasse, and Lindau's dwelling on Sigismundstrasse are all gone as well. The emperor's city castle was destroyed during World War II; the remainders were torn down by the East German government in 1950. It is being rebuilt today (the Royal Library on Unter den Linden was rebuilt as well). Even the American Church at Nollendorfplatz was obliterated by Allied bombs.

The only edifice remaining from the time when Twain lived in Berlin is the Brandenburg Gate. Today, however, an American congregation meets in Berlin again, still in Schöneberg, in a neogothic, red brick church with a tall steeple, just a few hundred yards away from Twain's very first apartment on Körnerstrasse.

And one descendant of the von Versen family is also to be found in Berlin today: Miriam von Versen, who owns a gallery for jewelry and accessories at 85 Auguststrasse, not far from the residence at Mauerstrasse, where Twain's cousin Alice lived with her husband, and where the writer himself had dinner with the Kaiser. Miriam's great-great-grandfather was the brother of Maximilian von Versen, Twain's "little General." So life goes on.

MARK TWAIN'S TRAVEL LETTERS FROM 1891–92
The Chicago Daily Tribune, April 3, 1892

BERLIN – THE CHICAGO OF EUROPE

I feel lost in Berlin. It has no resemblance to the city I had supposed it was. There was once a Berlin which I would have known, from descriptions in books—the Berlin of the last century and the beginning of the present one: a dingy city in a marsh, with rough streets, muddy and lantern-lighted, dividing straight rows of ugly houses all alike, compacted into blocks as square and plain and uniform and monotonous and serious as so many dry-goods boxes. But that Berlin has disappeared. It seems to have disappeared totally, and left no sign. The bulk of the Berlin of today has about it no suggestion of a former period. The site it stands on has traditions and a history, but the city itself has no traditions and no history. It is a new city; the newest I have ever seen. Chicago would seem venerable beside it; for there are many old-looking districts in Chicago, but not many in Berlin. The main mass of the city looks as if it had been built last week, the rest of it has a just perceptibly graver tone, and looks as if it might be six or even eight months old.

The next feature that strikes one is the spaciousness, the roominess of the city. There is no other city, in any country, whose streets are so generally wide. Berlin is not merely a city of wide streets, it is the city of wide streets. As a wide-street city it has never had its equal, in any age of the world. "Unter den Linden" is three streets in one; the Potsdamer Strasse is bordered on both sides by sidewalks which are themselves wider than some of the historic thoroughfares of the old European capitals; there seem to be no lanes or alleys; there are no short cuts; here and there, where several important streets empty into a common center, that center's circumference is of a magnitude calculated to bring that word spaciousness into your mind again. The park in the middle of the city is so huge that it calls up that expression once more.

The next feature that strikes one is the straightness of the streets. The short ones haven't so much as a waver in them; the long ones stretch out to prodigious distances and then tilt a little to the right or left, then stretch out on another immense reach as straight as a ray of light. A result of this arrangement is that at night Berlin is an inspiring sight to see. Gas and the electric light are employed with a wasteful liberality, and so, wherever one goes, he has always double ranks of brilliant lights stretching far down into the night on every hand, with here and there a wide and splendid constellation of them spread out over an intervening "platz," and between the interminable double procession of street lamps one has the swarming and darting cab lamps, a lively and pretty addition to the fine spectacle, for they counterfeit the rush and confusion and sparkle of an invasion of fireflies.

There is one other noticeable feature—the absolutely level surface of the site of Berlin. Berlin, to recapitulate, is newer to the eye than is any other city, and also blonder of complexion and tidier; no other city has such an air of roominess, freedom from crowding; no other city has so many straight streets; and with Chicago it contests the chromo for flatness of surface and for phenomenal swiftness of growth. Berlin is the European Chicago. The two cities have about the same population—say a million and a half. I cannot speak in exact terms, because I only know what Chicago's population was week before last; but at that time it was about a million and a half. Fifteen years ago Berlin and Chicago were large cities, of course, but neither of them was the giant it now is.

But now the parallels fail. Only parts of Chicago are stately and beautiful, whereas all of Berlin is stately and substantial, and it is not merely in parts but uniformly beautiful. There are buildings in Chicago that are architecturally finer than any in Berlin, I think, but what I have just said above is still true. These two flat cities would lead the world for phenomenal good health if London were out of the way. As it is, London leads by a point or two. Berlin's death rate is only nineteen in the thousand. Fourteen years ago the rate was a third higher.

Berlin is a surprise in a great many ways—in a multitude of ways, to speak strongly and be exact. It seems to be the most governed city in the world, but one must admit that it also seems to be the best governed. Method and system are observable on every hand—in great things, in little things, in all details, of whatsoever size. And it is not method and system on paper, and there an end—it is method and system in practice. It has a rule for everything, and puts the rule in force; puts it in force against the poor and powerful alike, without favor or prejudice. It deals with great matters and minute particulars with equal faithfulness, and with a plodding and painstaking diligence and persistency, which compel admiration—and sometimes regret. There are several taxes, and they are collected quarterly. Collected is the word; they are not merely levied, they are collected—every time. This makes light taxes. It is in cities and countries where a considerable part of the community shirk payment that taxes have to be lifted to a burdensome rate. Here the police keep coming, calmly and patiently, until you pay your tax. They charge you 5 or 10 cents per visit after the first call. By experiment you will find that they will presently collect that money.

In one respect the 1,500,000 of Berlin's population are like a family: the head of this large family knows the names of its several members, and where the said members are located, and when and where they were born, and what they do for a living, and what their religious brand is. Whoever comes to Berlin must furnish these particulars to the police immediately; moreover, if he knows how long he is going to stay, he must say so. If he takes a house he will be taxed on the rent and taxed also on his income. He will not be asked what his income is, and so he may save some lies for home consumption. The police will estimate his income from the house rent he pays, and tax him on that basis.

Duties on imported articles are collected with inflexible fidelity, be the sum large or little; but the methods are gentle, prompt, and full of the spirit of accommodation. The postman attends to the whole matter for you, in cases where the article comes by mail, and you have no trouble and suffer no inconvenience. The other day a friend of mine was informed that there was a package in the post-office for him, containing a lady's silk belt with gold clasp, and a gold chain to hang a bunch of keys on. In his first agitation he was going to try to bribe the postman to chalk it through, but acted upon his sober second thought and allowed the matter to take its proper and regular course. In a little while the postman brought the package and made these several collections: duty on the silk belt, 7 1/2 cents; duty on the gold chain, 10 cents; charge for fetching the package, 5 cents. These devastating imposts are exacted for the protection of German home industries.

The calm, quiet, courteous, cussed persistence of the police is the most admirable thing I have encountered on this side. They undertook to persuade me to send and get a passport for a Swiss maid whom we had brought with us, and at the end of six weeks of patient, tranquil, angelic daily effort they succeeded. I was not intending to give them trouble, but I was lazy and I thought they would get tired. Meanwhile they probably thought I would be the one. It turned out just so.

One is not allowed to build unstable, unsafe, or unsightly houses in Berlin; the result is this comely and conspicuously stately city, with its security from conflagrations and breakdowns. It is built of architectural Gibraltars. The building commissioners inspect while the building is going up. It has been found that this is better than to wait till it falls down. These people are full of whims. One is not allowed to cram poor folk into cramped and dirty tenement houses. Each individual must have just so many cubic feet of room-space, and sanitary inspections are systematic and frequent.

Everything is orderly. The fire brigade march in rank, curiously uniformed, and so grave is their demeanor that they look like a Salvation Army under conviction of sin. People tell me that when a fire alarm is sounded, the firemen assemble calmly, answer to their names when the roll is called, then proceed to the fire. There they are ranked up, military fashion, and told off in detachments by the chief, who parcels out to the detachments the several parts of the work which they are to undertake in putting out that fire. This is all done with low-voiced propriety, and strangers think these people are working a funeral. As a rule, the fire is confined to a single floor in these great masses of bricks and masonry, and consequently there is little or no interest attaching to a fire here for the rest of the occupants of the house.

There is abundance of newspapers in Berlin, and there was also a newsboy, but he died. At intervals of half a mile on the thoroughfares there are booths, and it is at these that you buy your papers. There are plenty of theaters, but they do not advertise in a loud way. There are no big posters of any kind, and the display of vast type and of pictures of actors and performance framed on a big scale and done in rainbow colors is a thing unknown. If the big show bills existed there would be no place to exhibit them; for there are no poster fences, and one would not be allowed to disfigure dead walls with them. Unsightly things are forbidden here; Berlin is a rest to the eye.

And yet the saunterer can easily find out what is going

on at the theaters. All over the city, at short distances apart, there are neat round pillars eighteen feet high and about as thick as a hogshead, and on these the little black and white theater bills and other notices are posted. One generally finds a group around each pillar reading these things. There are plenty of things in Berlin worth importing to America. It is these that I have particularly wished to make a note of. When Buffalo Bill was here his biggest poster was probably not larger than the top of an ordinary trunk.

There is a multiplicity of clean and comfortable horse-cars, but whenever you think you know where a car is going to you would better stop ashore, because that car is not going to that place at all. The car routes are marvelously intricate, and often the drivers get lost and are not heard of for years. The signs on the cars furnish no details as to the course of the journey; they name the end of it, and then experiment around to see how much territory they can cover before they get there. The conductor will collect your fare over again every few miles, and give you a ticket which he hasn't apparently kept any record of, and you keep it till an inspector comes aboard by and by and tears a corner off it (which he does not keep), then you throw the ticket away and get ready to buy another. Brains are of no value when you are trying to navigate Berlin in a horse-car. When the ablest of Brooklyn's editors was here on a visit he took a horse-car in the early morning, and wore it out trying to go to a point in the center of the city. He was on board all day and spent many dollars in fares, and then did not arrive at the place, which he had started to go to. This is the most thorough way to see Berlin, but it is also the most expensive.

But there are excellent features about the car system, nevertheless. The car will not stop for you to get on or off, except at certain places a block or two apart where there is a sign to indicate that that is a halting-station. This system saves many bones. There are twenty places inside the car; when these seats are filled, no more can enter. Four or five persons may stand on each platform—the law decrees the number—and when these standing places are all occupied the next applicant is refused. As there is no crowding, and as no rowdyism is allowed, women stand on the platforms as well as the men; they often stand there when there are vacant seats inside, for these places are comfortable, there being little or no jolting.

A native tells me that when the first car was put on, thirty or forty years ago, the public had such a terror of it that they didn't feel safe inside of it, or outside either. They made the company keep a man at every crossing with a red flag in his hand. Nobody would travel in the car except convicts on the way to the gallows. This made business in only one direction, and the car had to go back light. To save the company, the city government transferred the convict cemetery to the other end of the line. This made traffic in both directions and kept the company from going under. This sounds like some of the information which traveling foreigners are furnished with in America. To my mind it has a doubtful ring about it.

The first-class cab is neat and trim, and has leather-cushion seats and a swift horse. The second-class cab is an ugly and lubberly vehicle, and is always old. It seems a strange thing that they have never built any new ones. Still, if such a thing were done everybody that had time to flock would flock to see it, and that would make a crowd, and the police do not like crowds and disorder here. If there were an earthquake in Berlin the police would take charge of it and conduct it in that sort of orderly way that would make you think it was a prayer meeting. That is what an earthquake generally ends in, but this one would be different from those others; it would be kind of soft and self-contained, like a Republican praying for a mugwump.

For a course (a quarter of an hour or less), one pays 25 cents in a first-class cab, and 15 cents in a second-class. The first-class will take you along faster, for the second-class horse is old—always old—as old as his cab, some authorities say—and ill-fed and weak. He has been a first-class once, but has been degraded to second class for long and faithful service.

Still, he must take you as far for 15 cents as the other horse takes you for 25. If he can't do his fifteen-minute distance in fifteen minutes, he must still do the distance for the 15 cents. Any stranger can check the distance off—by means of the most curious map I am acquainted with. It is issued by the city government and can be bought in any shop for a trifle. In it every street is sectioned off like a string of long beads of different colors. Each long bead represents a minute's travel, and when you have covered fifteen of the beads you have got your money's worth. This map of Berlin is a gay-colored maze, and looks like pictures of the circulation of the blood.

The streets are very clean. They are kept so—not by prayer and talk and the other New York methods, but by daily and hourly work with scrapers and brooms; and when an asphalted street has been tidily scraped after a rain or a light snowfall, they scatter clean sand over it. This saves some of the horses from falling down. In fact, this is a city government which seems to stop at no expense where the public convenience, comfort, and health are concerned—except in one detail. That is the naming of the streets and the numbering of the houses. Sometimes the name of a street will change in the middle of a block. You will not find it out till you get to the next corner and discover the new name on the wall, and of course you don't know just when the change happened.

The names are plainly marked on the corners—on all the corners—there are no exceptions. But the numbering of the houses—there has never been anything like it since original chaos. It is not possible that it was done by this wise city government. At first one thinks it was done by an idiot; but there is too much variety about it for that; an idiot could not think of so many different ways of making confusion and propagating blasphemy. The numbers run up one side the street and down the other. That is endurable, but the rest isn't. They often use one number for three or four houses—and sometimes they put the number on only one of the houses and let you guess at the others. Sometimes they put a number on a house—4, for instance—then put 4a, 4b, 4c, on the succeeding houses, and one becomes old and decrepit before he finally arrives at 5. A result of this systemless system is that when you are at No. 1 in a street you haven't any idea how far it may be to No. 150; it may be only six or eight blocks, it may be a couple of miles. Frederick Street is long, and is one of the great thoroughfares. The other day a man put up his money behind the assertion that there were more refreshment places in that street than numbers on the houses—and he won. There were 254 numbers and 257 refreshment places. Yet as I have said, it is a long street.

But the worst feature of all this complex business is that in Berlin the numbers do not travel in any one direction; no, they travel along until they get to 50 or 60, perhaps, then suddenly you find yourself up in the hundreds—140, maybe; the next will be 139—then you perceive by that sign that the numbers are now traveling toward you from the opposite direction. They will keep that sort of insanity up as long as you travel that street; every now and then the numbers will turn and run the other way. As a rule, there is an arrow under the number, to show by the direction of its flight, which way the numbers are proceeding. There are a good many suicides in Berlin; I have seen six reported in one day. There is always a deal of learned and laborious arguing and ciphering going on as to the cause of this state of things. If they will set to work and number their houses in a rational way perhaps they will find out what was the matter.

More than a month ago Berlin began to prepare to celebrate Professor Virchow's seventieth birthday. When the birthday arrived, the middle of October, it seemed to me that all the world of science arrived with it; deputation after deputation came, bringing the homage and reverence of far cities and centers of learning, and during the whole of a long day the hero of it sat and received such witness of his greatness as has seldom been vouchsafed to any man in any walk of life in any time, ancient or modern. These demonstrations were continued in one form or another day after day, and were presently merged in similar demonstrations to his twin in science and achievement, Professor Helmholtz, whose seventieth birthday is separated from Virchow's by only about three weeks; so nearly as this did these two extraordinary men come to being born together. Two such births have seldom signalized a single year in human history.

But perhaps the final and closing demonstration was peculiarly grateful to them. This was a commers given in their honor the other night by 1,000 students. It was held in a huge hall, very long and very lofty, which had five galleries, far above everybody's head, which were crowded with ladies—400 or 500, I judged. It was beautifully decorated with clustered flags and various ornamental devices, and was brilliantly lighted. On the spacious floor of this place were ranged, in files, innumerable tables, seating twenty-four persons each, extending from one end of the great hall clear to the other, and with narrow aisles between the files. In the center on one side was a high and tastefully decorated platform twenty or thirty feet long, with a long table on it, behind which sat the half-dozen chiefs of the choir of the commers in the rich medieval costumes of as many different college corps. Behind these youths a band of musicians was concealed. On the floor directly in front of this platform were half a dozen tables which were distinguished from the outlying continent of tables by being covered instead of left naked. Of these the central table was reserved for the two heroes of the occasion and twenty particularly eminent professors of the Berlin University, and the other covered tables were for the occupancy of a hundred less distinguished professors.

I was glad to be honored with a place at the table of the two heroes of the occasion, although I was not really learned enough to deserve it. Indeed, there was a pleasant strangeness in being in such company; to be thus associated with twenty-three men who forget more every day than I ever knew. Yet there was nothing embarrassing about it, because loaded men and empty ones look about alike. I knew that to that multitude there I was a professor. It required but little art to catch the ways and attitude of those men and imitate them, and I had no difficulty in looking as much like a professor as anybody there.

We arrived early; so early that only Professors Virchow and Helmholtz and a dozen guests of the special tables were ahead of us, and 300 or 400 students. But people were arriving in floods now, and within fifteen minutes all but the special tables were occupied, and the great house was crammed, the aisles included. It was said that there were 4,000 men present. It was a most animated scene, there is no doubt about that; it was a stupendous beehive. At each end of each table stood a corps student in the uniform of his corps. These quaint costumes are of brilliant colored silks and velvets, with sometimes a high plumed hat, sometimes a broad Scotch cap, with a great plume wound about it, sometimes—oftenest—a little shallow silk cap on the tip of the crown, like an inverted saucer; sometimes the pantaloons are snow-white, sometimes of other colors; the boots in all cases come up well above the knee; and in all cases also white gauntlets are worn; the sword is a rapier with a bowl-shaped guard for the hand, painted in several colors. Each corps has a uniform of its own, and all are of rich material, brilliant in color, and exceedingly picturesque; for they are survivals of the vanished costumes of the Middle Ages, and they reproduce for us the time when men were beautiful to look at. The student who stood guard at our end of the table was of grave countenance and great frame and grace of form, and he was doubtless an accurate reproduction, clothes and all, of some ancestor of his of two or three centuries ago—a reproduction as far as the outside, the animal man, goes, I mean.

As I say, the place was now crowded. The nearest aisle was packed with students standing up, and they made a fence, which shut off the rest of the house from view. As far down this fence as you could see all these wholesome young faces were turned in one direction, all these intent and worshiping eyes were centered upon one spot—the place where Virchow and Helmholtz sat. The boys seemed lost to everything, unconscious of their own existence; they devoured these two intellectual giants with their eyes, they feasted upon them, and the worship that was in their hearts shone in their faces. It seemed to me that I would rather be flooded with a glory like that—instinct with sincerity, innocent of self-seeking—than win a hundred battles and break a million hearts.

There was a big mug of beer in front of each of us, and more to come when wanted. There was also a quarto pamphlet containing the words of the songs to be sung. After the names of the officers of the feast were these words in large type: "Wahrend des Kommerses herrscht allgemeiner Burgfriede."

I was not able to translate this to my satisfaction, but a professor helped me out. This was his explanation: The students in uniform belong to different college corps; not all students belong to corps; none join the corps except those who enjoy fighting. The corps students fight duels with swords every week, one corps challenging another corps to furnish a certain number of duelists for the occasion, and it is only on this battlefield that students of different corps exchange courtesies. In common life they do not drink with each other or speak. The above line now translates itself: there is truce during the Commers, war is laid aside and fellowship takes its place.

Now the performance began. The concealed band played a piece of martial music; then there was a pause. The students on the platform rose to their feet, the middle one gave a toast to the Emperor, then all the house rose, mugs in hand. At the call "One, two, three!" all glasses were drained and then brought down with a slam on the tables in unison. The result was as good an imitation of thunder as I have ever heard. From now on, during an hour, there was singing, in mighty chorus.

During each interval between songs a number of the special guests—the professors—arrived. There seemed to be some signal whereby the students on the platform were made aware that a professor had arrived at the remote door of entrance; for you would see them suddenly rise to their feet, strike an erect military attitude, then draw their swords; the swords of all their brethren standing guard at the innumerable tables would flash from their scabbards and be held aloft—a handsome spectacle. Three clear bugle notes would ring out, then all these swords would come down with a crash, twice repeated, on the tables, and be uplifted and held aloft again; then in the distance you would see the gay uniforms and uplifted swords of a guard of honor clearing the way and conducting the guest down to his place.

The songs were stirring, the immense out-pour from young life and young lungs, the crash of swords and the thunder of the beer-mugs gradually worked a body up to what seemed the last possible summit of excitement. It surely seemed to me that I had reached that summit, that I had reached my limit, and that there was no higher lift desirable for me. When apparently the last eminent guest had long ago taken his place, again those three bugle blasts rang out and once more the swords leaped from their scabbards. Who might this late comer be? Nobody was interested to inquire. Still, indolent eyes were turned toward the distant entrance; we saw the silken gleam and the lifted swords of a guard of honor plowing through the remote crowds. Then we saw that end of the house rising to its feet; saw it rise abreast the advancing guard all along, like a wave. This supreme honor had been offered to no one before. Then there was an excited whisper at our table—"Mommsen!"—and the whole house rose. Rose and shouted and stamped and clapped, and banged the beer-mugs. Just simply a storm! Then the little man with his long hair and Emersonian face edged his way past us and took his seat. I could have touched him with my hand—Mommsen!—think of it!

This was one of those immense surprises that can happen only a few times in one's life. I was not dreaming of him; he was to me only a giant myth, a world-shadowing specter, not a reality. The surprise of it all can be only comparable to a man's suddenly coming upon Mont Blanc, with its awful form towering into the sky, when he didn't suspect he was in its neighborhood. I would have walked a great many miles to get a sight of him, and here he was, without trouble or tramp or cost of any kind. Here he was, clothed in a Titanic deceptive modesty, which made him look like other men. Here he was, carrying the Roman world and all the Caesars in his hospitable skull, and doing it as easily as that other luminous vault, the skull of the universe, carries the Milky Way and the constellations.

One of the professors said that once upon a time an American young lady was introduced to Mommsen, and found herself badly scared and speechless. She dreaded to see his mouth unclose, for she was expecting him to choose a subject several miles above her comprehension, and didn't suppose he could get down to the world that other people lived in; but when his remark came, her terrors disappeared.

"Well, how do you do? Have you read Howells's last book? I think it's his best."

The active ceremonies of the evening closed with the speeches of welcome delivered by two students and the replies made by Professors Virchow and Helmholtz.

Virchow has long been a member of the city government of Berlin. He works as hard for the city as does any other Berlin Alderman, and gets the same pay—nothing. I don't know that we in America could venture to ask our most illustrious citizen to serve in a Board of Aldermen, and if we might venture it I am not positively sure that we could elect him. But here the municipal system is such that the best men in the city consider it an honor to serve gratis as Aldermen, and the people have the good sense to prefer these men and to elect them year after year. As a result Berlin is a thoroughly well-governed city. It is a free city; its affairs are not meddled with by the state; they are managed by its own citizens, and after methods of their own devising.

The Sunday supplement of National-Zeitung, *November 15, 1891*

National-Zeitung
Mark Twain in Berlin

November 15, 1891

Of the three American humorists whose works have been well translated for a German audience, John Habberton currently commands our interest. The long series of booklets, in which he relates the fate of Helena's little children, Bob and Teddy, from their tenderest young age till they're bigger nuisances, has the same fate as it makes its way through thousands of houses: it causes laughter—happy, hearty, resounding, contagious laughter. John Habberton was a welcome guest wherever people met him, and he attributed this success to the photographic and microscopic fidelity with which he describes a child's heart and soul and the thoughts that fill a child's little head. Incidentally, in order to be able to do that, one must see with a child's eyes and feel with a child's heart.

Bret Harte's successes in Germany before him were no less warm, though via other means. First there was the world into which Bret led us, one foreign to us and so all the more captivating. Like the effect that Indian stories have on a child's world, his accounts of the pioneers' struggles with the wilderness and with each other awakened our fantasy. Not just the subject, but also his treatment soon awakened our sense of wonder. If he bluntly presented the manpower required to begin a new settlement and did not withhold the fact that the prisons almost exclusively contributed to that, and that in any case the bankruptcy of an entire life was necessary before one could afford the trip to the California mines, he tried all the harder to illustrate that even the most depraved individual's humanity cannot be fully destroyed.

Though course, his accounts also strike an emotional chord, and we really see how the group develops from out of the swamp and into a civilization in the hard school of life. The raw background of that life is what makes every human emotion twice as striking.

Mark Twain's humor is fundamentally different from Habberton's and Bret Harte's. In him we have the father of an entire literary school, who educates his nation by laying bare its weaknesses. His weapons are mockery and scorn; through intentional and recognizable exaggeration, he reveals the weaknesses of his fellow countrymen, who are used to measuring everything against a standard of gigantic proportions. He is a satirist who has claimed Don Quixote as his example. But while one laughs at his exaggerations, one immediately recognizes the legitimate kernel of criticism disguised in this peculiar form. Unlike the others, who are predominantly authors who view the novella as their own special field, Mark Twain remains a journalist, which will not change just because he has achieved significant success with a series of stories. Even in these, he portrays daily occurrences. What happens is and remains the starting point for his accounts. One of his most famous works, *Innocents Abroad,* describes the travels of a large number of Americans to Palestine and gives him double the opportunity to crack his whip, once at his fellow countrymen and travel companions, and then at the country and people he meets along the way.

Mark Twain has been in Berlin for a few weeks now. Those who know him only from his descriptions of the Kentucky editors' office—where the editor deals with his subscribers only armed to the teeth, with a revolver in his back pocket, a Bowie knife in his belt—might imagine him as a strong, sinewy man of the familiar New England type, swift and quick to judge, an energetic negotiator, perhaps even reckless. And so it is all the more surprising to find him to be the exact opposite of what one might expect.

Mark Twain—whose given name is Samuel Clemens—came to Berlin with his wife and children, very musical adolescent young ladies and gentlemen, to give them the opportunity to hear good music. They say that Berlin is the place to go if one values good instrumental music, as it is well known that Berlin offers more opportunity than any other place in the world. And so he has settled in for a long stay, on as quiet a street as possible, Körnerstrasse, where he is leasing a furnished apartment that is large by American standards, complete with furniture and decorative pictures, right down to the last pot in the kitchen and napkin in the cupboard. There he carries on his studies which, as one might imagine and which he does not deny, might very likely appear in some little piece on Berlin. He is a charming host: a man of medium build, a somewhat weak body topped by a head framed by thick, bushy, and long, graying hair, whose moustache, though, still clearly shows its former dark blond color. The eyebrows arch powerfully; the lips are thin and finely chiseled; one sees the philosopher in him at first glance. He extends his left hand in greeting: the right won't obey him, he grumbles, though he soaked it in the hot springs at Aix-les-Bains for eight long weeks, to cure his rheumatism. He hopes that he'll mend under Professor Gerhard's care. In the meantime, he's managing it like Echternach's hopping procession: one step forward each day and then two steps back. He complains most of all about being forbidden to write his own entries in his notebook.

His arm's affliction stems from overwork. Beginning in February of this year, he wrote a novella for 72 days straight, uninterrupted, which will soon be published in a series of English and American papers, under the title *The American Claimant*. In it, he castigates the increasing tendency of unions to make demands for fortune, titles, and property, an obsession that never really stopped after the fall of Tichborne and has increased dramatically of late.

"How long do you plan to stay in Berlin?" I asked him, before finding out that he had settled in.

"Until your taxes drive me away," was his slow and deliberate reply, revealing the business-minded American within the writer as well. He has not been in Berlin very long, but he has already learned of the new income-tax law on its way, which includes a section aimed specifically at foreigners. It comforted him to learn that he can stay for some time unmolested, before his gold-dollars will be taxed into mark pieces. "I'm glad about that," he said, "because it eliminates a prejudice that I had. I was told that I would be taxed immediately. Not that I would have any objections because of the money, God forbid. One spends so much on trips, so that really doesn't play any role. But it's about the bad impression. A foreigner should not be subject to tax at all, neither for brief nor longer stays. He is neither a nuisance, nor does he wish to become one; on the contrary, he wants to be agreeable and is, insofar as he gives something to the country. If he does become a nuisance, however, the laws suffice to bring him back to his senses. But generally, he should be a welcome guest."

He paused momentarily, when a large dog barked on the street. "Do you hear that?" he asked, "That dog. I know that one. He's a bassist and directs the choir. Now he'll wait a bit, and then he'll have company. Apparently there's an organized dog-choir-club on this street. Right, there's the second tenor, now. I am, as my presence in Berlin shows, a music fan. But I was not prepared for this pleasure on this quiet street. To return to the taxation of foreigners, that is what I would propose: Forgive foreigners all taxes and tax the dogs instead. That accomplishes two things. You attract foreigners, which you need, and you get rid of the dogs, which you don't need." Meanwhile, he had walked to the window. "There's a red one, running around and threatening the children with its wild jumping. Someone put a muzzle on its snout that hinders its eating, but not its bite."

"You don't seem to be a fan of dogs," I suggested shyly, picturing his descriptions of how differences of opinion are resolved in Kentucky.

But I was less interested in what he said than in how he said it. While he spoke, he paced slowly back and forth, without sitting, for an entire hour. Every word came out slowly, deliberately, with pauses between them. There are few people who speak so slowly, and one could tell that he is used to shaping each word, making each ready for print, I might add, before uttering it.

He has not seen much of Berlin yet; his affliction has kept him from going out much. But what he has seen has been a great joy. He has not had much cause to criticize—i.e., has found little that has annoyed him.

"That," I remarked, "will make your book about Berlin difficult."

"Then such a book remains best unwritten," was his reply. "Nothing seems more unjustified or damnable than when someone expresses harsh judgment, even in satiric form, because he's itching to hurt someone or because he thinks his crude manner will bring joy to others. I would even distance myself from criticism if I thought the one being criticized wouldn't want to hear what I thought of him and wouldn't care. Life is too valuable to waste on unfruitful endeavors. Why waste good paper, good ink, and time best spent on other things, on nothing. Especially someone traveling to a foreign country to express his opinion about his perceptions should only do so with the intention and conviction that people understand it like the author means it and get the impression that he respects the justified peculiarities of the country in question. But that is exactly what bothers us Americans so often—if I may be so bold—when you Europeans come over to us and enjoy our hospitality and protection under our laws, but then describe the trip with unmistakable arrogance, disparaging whatever springs into view and seems foreign, without even trying to get to the bottom of it. Anyone who goes to a foreign country and reaps the benefits of the establishment provided first for its citizens should consider himself to be a guest…"

"Regarding Berlin," he continued after a brief pause, "it has made a particularly pleasant impression on me, and I only regret that I did not see it 25 years ago, when I passed nearby during my trip to Palestine. But who thought back then that one had to see Berlin. Munich and Dresden and Cologne were on the travel route, and whoever saw those three cities imagined he really knew Germany through and through. Now I have no basis for comparison, which I find to be a tremendous loss. But what I do see is wonderful. People must use excellent coal here, as the houses are not covered with a thick layer of soot and smoke. And what beautiful architecture there is in the various streets, with alternating balconies and additions lined up one after another; yet far more impressive and agreeable is the city's light face, the bright colors, the friendly, welcoming tone of the facades. When the sun shines on them at noon, its glittering rays flashing over it, lingering there and illuminating the entire long street in joyful, golden splendor, that is a sight one never tires of seeing—one that is pleasant and agreeable to the eyes and the heart."

After a short while, he returned to the subject of our taxes. "If I really think about it," he laughed as he recalled the experience, "I can't find it so bad that foreigners staying in Germany are taxed.

Because it's much worse in England; there they tax the foreigners if they're writers, even if they have never set foot on English ground. My works were published in London, too. Last year, I received from my publisher a request to notify the English tax office of how much I benefited from my books published in London and to pay taxes on it. My publisher tried in vain to establish that there was not the least shred of law to support this; he testified and then sent me the entire file. We studied the tax code forwards and backwards, and backwards and forwards, three or four times, to figure out under which tax code my obligation might fall. In the end, we found the section, number, and page—with no room for error—my writing was classified as the product of gas."

"As gas?"

"As gas," he replied. "With no room for error. That seems impossible, but that's how it was. What they were thinking in London, I just don't know. Someone probably threw some dice to see which tax chapter would cover it. Fate was kind to me. It classified the effect of my book under explosive materials. Even if no one else did, at least we, my friends and I, laughed about it."

"And you did not complain?"

"No," he replied, "My publisher wanted to and asked me to. But what action should I take against those who so exquisitely increased my knowledge of England? If all American writers had gotten together to appeal, I would not have excluded myself. But to go to court alone and to bother with or lose my head over the trickiness of English justice? No, I'd rather pay and be happy to be done with the matter at once and not have anything to keep me from my work. There's nothing better than peace and calm."

He said all of that in the same steady, deliberate, contemplative tone, rising up and lowering down. Today he did not act like the great humorist he is known to be, but as one who is wise to the world and a philosopher of high moral fiber. We do know that he does not want to simply entertain his public but to educate as well, and that his writing takes on a certain weight; in this sense, it might be considered a boon to America that his success as a writer has not kept him away from his journalistic activity. Though he stopped lining up type from the typesetter's box thirty-five years ago and gave up his place at the editor's desk twenty years ago, he continues to appear occasionally in the channel of newspapers that spread throughout the land like millions of tiny streams, castigating and thereby urging readers to reflect and change their ways. But when he writes about Berlin some day, we'll be doubly interested to see what sketches his current sojourn here might yield.

—Max Horwitz

Dienstag, 24. November.

Stunde ist nicht ferngeblieben; seine heiße Sehnsucht nach Versöhnung mit Graf Heldberg, nach einem letzten Wiedersehen mit seiner Gemahlin, hat ihn zur rechten Zeit hierher geführt."

(Fortsetzung folgt.)

—(**Mark Twain.**) Wie man weiß, beherbergt Berlin seit kurzem als Gast Mark Twain, den berühmtesten amerikanischen Humoristen, den zur Zeit wohl überhaupt hervorragendsten satirischen Schriftsteller. Twain, mit seinem bürgerlichen Namen Samuel Langhore Clemens, ist in Florida im Staate Missouri am 30. November 1835 geboren, feiert also binnen wenigen Tagen hier in Berlin seinen sechsundfünfzigsten Geburtstag. Wir haben, schreibt der „B. B.-C.", schon einmal an dieser Stelle bei anderer Gelegenheit ausgeführt, eine wie große Summe von Intelligenz und Geist sich in England und Amerika gerade in dem Stande der „Reporter" vereinigt findet. Gleich Stanley, gleich dem mit göttlichem Humor begnadeten Charles Dickens ist auch Mark Twain aus den Kreisen der Reporter hervorgegangen. Allerdings reicht der Beginn seiner Zeitungs-Carrière noch weiter zurück. Er war ganz zuerst, was man in Amerika „devil" nennt, nämlich Druckereijunge, und hatte als solcher die üblichen Handlangerdienste sowie das Ueberbringen der Manuscripte zu verrichten. Wer diesem kleinen, druckerschwarzen armen „Teufel" damals gesagt hätte, daß man ihm dereinst seine eigenen Manuscripte mit schwerem Golde aufwiegen werde?! Vom „devil" schwang er sich zum Setzer in der Officin einer californischen Zeitung auf, vertauschte aber bald die Setzlinie und den Winkelhaken mit dem Sentblei des Lootsen. Auf den Mississippi-Stamern machte er als solcher zahlreiche Fahrten und, wenn es auch als bekannt vorausgesetzt werden kann, so mag hier doch noch einmal daran erinnert sein, daß sein so weltberühmt gewordener Schriftstellername in Verbindung mit seinen Lootsen-Erlebnissen steht. „Mark twain", wörtlich: „Markir zweimal", bedeutet in der Sprache der Schiffsleute des Mississippi „Zwei Faden tief". Nachdem Mark Twain in Nevada Journalist geworden und mehrere Jahre in Virginia City an der „Entreprise" gearbeitet hatte, ging er als Special-Correspondent nach den Sandwichsinseln. Interessant ist es, daß Twain, welcher später eine unerschöpfliche Goldmine in seinem Talent entdecken sollte, auch als Silbergräber lange Zeit in den Minen des Territoriums Nevada die Spitzhacke geschwungen hat, allerdings ohne Erfolg. Im Jahre 1867 trat ein Ereigniß ein, welches für Twain's ganzes Leben von entscheidender Bedeutung war. Eine Anzahl mehrerer Hundert Amerikaner machte auf dem Dampfer „Quaker City" eine Vergnügungsfahrt ins Mittelmeer bis nach Aegypten und Palästina. Twain schloß sich dieser Reisegesellschaft an und schilderte, nach Amerika zurückgekehrt, ihre Erlebnisse in dem Buche „Innocents abroad" (Unschuldige in der Fremde") mit hinreißendem Humor. Das Werk machte seinen Verfasser in den Vereinigten Staaten mit einem Schlage zum populären Mann. Hunderttausende von Exemplaren wurden in ein bis zwei Jahren davon verkauft. Heute besitzt Twain, welcher für gewöhnlich in Harford in Connecticut lebt, dort ein eigenes, sehr schön und behaglich eingerichtetes Haus. Er bildet auch insofern eine interessante, echt amerikanische Erscheinung, als er nicht nur Schriftsteller, sondern auch gleichzeitig Verleger seiner eigenen Werke und derjenigen anderer Autoren ist. So erschien z. B. in seinem Verlage die Selbstbiographie des Generals Grant, welche der ehemalige Präsident Nordamerika's auf seinem Krankenbette, ein sterbensmüder Mann, schrieb, um seiner Familie ein Vermögen hinterlassen zu können. Das Buch, welchem natürlich ganz Amerika ein fieberhaftes Interesse entgegenbrachte, trug den Angehörigen Grant's 300 000 Dollars, also zwölfmalhunderttausend Mark Reingewinn und dem zarten Verleger eine gleich große Summe ein. Twain weiß stets das Angenehme mit dem Nützlichen zu verbinden, und wenn er jetzt nach Berlin gekommen ist, um hier einige Monate zu verweilen und das Leben der Reichshauptstadt zu studiren, so benutzt er gleich die Gelegenheit, um für die amerikanische „World" eine Anzahl Berliner Feuilletons und Schilderungen zu schreiben, denen man mit großer Spannung entgegensehen wird. Einen sehr bedeutenden Theil der Kosten seines hiesigen Aufenthaltes wird Mark Twain dadurch sicherlich wieder herausschlagen, denn er ist gegenwärtig in Amerika der bestbezahlte Schrift-

Mark Twain in Breslauer Morgenzeitung *of November 24, 1891*

Breslauer Morgenzeitung
Mark Twain

November 24, 1891

(Mark Twain). As you know, Berlin recently became host to Mark Twain, the most famous American humorist, currently the most outstanding satiric author of all. Twain, whose given name is Samuel Langhorne Clemens, was born on November 30, 1835, in the Missouri town of Florida, and will be celebrating his 56th birthday here in Berlin in a few days. "B. B. C." writes that we've had the opportunity once before to explain in this space what a huge sum of intelligence and intellect is to be found united in England and America under the profession of "Reporter." Like Stanley, like Charles Dickens with his gift of divine humor, Mark Twain also emerged from the ranks of reporters, though the beginning of his newspaper career reaches back even farther. At first he was what Americans call a "devil," namely a printer's apprentice, and as such performed the usual odd jobs and delivered manuscripts.

Who would have predicted then, to that poor little "devil," black with ink, that his manuscripts would one day be worth their weight in gold! He went from "devil" to typesetter for a Californian newspaper, but soon swapped his composing rule and stick for a ship pilot's plumbline. He piloted numerous Mississippi steamers, and presuming everyone is familiar with it already, let us remind the reader once again that his world-famous pen name is associated with his experience as a pilot. "Mark twain," literally, "Mark twice," means "Two fathoms deep," in the parlance of Mississippi boat crews. After Mark Twain became a journalist in Nevada and worked for many years at the "Entreprise" in Virginia City, he traveled to the Sandwich Islands [i.e. Hawaii] as a special correspondent.

It is interesting that Twain, who would later discover an inexhaustible gold mine in his own talent, also swung a pickax for a long while in the silver mines in Nevada territory, though without success. In 1867 came an event that would change the course of Twain's life. Several hundred Americans took a pleasure cruise aboard the steamer *Quaker City*, through the Mediterranean to Egypt and Palestine. Twain joined the tour and, upon returning home to America, described their experiences in the fantastically funny book *Innocents Abroad*. The book made its author instantly popular in the United States. Hundreds of thousands of copies were sold within one or two years. Today, Twain owns a beautiful and comfortably furnished home in Hartford, Connecticut, where he usually lives. He also represents an interesting, truly American phenomenon, in that he is not just an author, but also the publisher of his own works, as well as those of others.

Twain published General Grant's autobiography, for example, which the former North American president wrote on his deathbed, in order to leave behind some assets for his family. The book, which generated feverish excitement all over America, of course, netted Grant's family $300,000, or 1.2 million marks, and the smart publisher an equally large sum. Twain always knows how to combine what is entertaining with what is useful, and if he came to Berlin now to spend a few months here, studying life in the imperial capital, he's sure to use the opportunity to write a number of greatly anticipated Berlin *feuilletons* and characterizations for the American "world." In this manner, he's sure to cover a significant portion of the cost of his current sojourn, as he is currently the best-paid author in America. He earns about 800 marks for a single column!

While this is Twain's first time in Berlin, he has already been to Germany on more than one occasion. We remember what he wrote in such humorously exaggerated colors, of his expeditions through the Black Forest, his trips on the Neckar River, and the difficulty of the German language, in his book, *Tramp Abroad*. Just last summer, Twain stopped in Hannover and made an excursion to Friedrichsruh. What an interesting encounter that would have been, had chance brought the Prince and the famous American together. The former typesetter, pilot, and treasure hunter arrived in Berlin a few days ago, with his wife, grown children, and a French maid, and rented and furnished an entire floor for several months. His appearance immediately betrays this important figure. Atop a slight frame sits a magnificent, graying head with busy eyebrows over razor-sharp eyes.

Mark Twain is a Yankee from head to toe, and accordingly unshakably apathetic. Even if his house were on fire, he would not get up from his desk or even dry his quill on the blotter and set it aside, annoyed, until the firemen flooded the room with water. Apropos—for the time being, Mark Twain cannot even pick up a quill; he suffers from rheumatism in his right arm and hopes that here he can send the malady packing. His charming wife has become his secretary; he dictates to her daily, but he describes it to be "dreadfully difficult." He is not used to dictating at all and has always written down his own thoughts himself. Mark Twain speaks slowly and deliberately, as if considering each word one more time before uttering it. But don't expect him to let loose a little cavalcade of brilliance at every visit. On the contrary, he is serious, thrifty with his wit, not unwilling to waste it without reason.

For interviewers, the celebrated author proves to be a nut that is hard to crack. His short, terse answers withhold everything and could drive pencil-pushing journalists to despair. Twain embraces practical principles: "Interview me? Why? To publish something about it in the papers? But I can do a far better job of that myself!" Well informed sources estimate his worth at two million dollars. What treasures are yet to be found in that black, magic potion of ink! All it takes is a magic quill and a good dose of luck. Although Twain would like to live in seclusion here in Berlin—until now he has only paid visits to American Ambassador Phelps, and Misters von Boetticher and Rottenburg—he is understandably at the center of interest and attention of the English-American colony here, and he was also obliged to accept an invitation to a "Thanksgiving day" banquet taking place at the English House next week.

Incidentally, he is a moderate eater and an even more moderate drinker. We can also divulge that Twain's favorite German poet is Heinrich Heine and that he finds Berlin to be "terribly clean." Even Berlin's administration, as far as he has gotten to know it so far, has earned Mark Twain's warm praise. Only one other city can he compare to Berlin in this regard—Glasgow. Twain, who has also visited many theaters and public events in Berlin, recently took a tour in a second-class cab. What a delightful chapter about his "adventure in a Berlin taxi-cab, hauled by an alleged horse," might the great humorist already have in mind?!

Berliner Tageblatt with the Twain story, on January 14, 1892

Berliner Tageblatt
America in Berlin

Januar 14, 1892

Last night around 8 o'clock, those in Berlin's Wilhelmstrasse might have thought they were on Broadway in New York. American personalities, American conversations! The illusion was increased by the fog that cloaked the local buildings and shop signs in a white veil, leaving only the stream of people recognizable under the gas lanterns and electric lights, heading for a tall, gothic-domed entrance. In the large assembly room of the Young Men's Christian Association—as announced—the American humorist Mark Twain was to give a lecture, about the construction of an American church in Berlin, no less. At the moment, there is no such thing, but the construction is a favorite subject among the entire American colony, which shows its interest in the matter by appearing in unusually large numbers. Dr. Stuckenberg, the American preacher, did the evening's honors, supported by young men from the society. According to the program, Mark Twain's lecture was to be interspersed with singing and cello-playing by American artists.

I arrived rather early, as I like to watch an audience arrive and grow. And one hears all kinds of entertaining and educational things. Today, the generally English conversation set the right tone and Mark Twain mood, even for the few Germans scattered here and there, among the foreigners.

At first I saw only women—pretty, young women with eccentric hats, with feathers bobbing and red ribbons, and fine, narrow, interesting faces, and slender, graceful figures. Then individual men arrived; on the corner seats of each row, there were mostly correspondents from newspapers, and if they were German-tongued, Mark Twain's quiet, pause-ridden manner of speaking had them scratching their heads. Then the other men arrived, indeed the young Republican women near me were struck with reverence and delight at the sight of two "real" officers in uniform. The room was full; every head turned to the door. The vaulted, church-like room, usually reserved for worship, has probably never seen so much elegance and curiosity (or should I say excitement?), all at once. What would he be like? Look like? Everyone had read his work, but even among his fellow countrymen, few had ever seen him.

Then Dr. Stuckenberg led a tall, lean, white-haired man through the crowd, to the podium. A young American began to sing, and Mark Twain sat down and listened attentively to the song. I sat just a few feet from the podium and could observe the beloved humorist's every move. A pale, narrow, bold face under white, mane-like hair; small, dark, deep-set eyes twinkled under bushy, still-dark brows, then looked sharply observant into the distance; a curved nose with vaulted nostrils, a long, dark moustache over a quick-witted mouth and strong chin; atop a supple, nimble, elegant figure.

Shhhh! Hush! He's starting to talk. Mr. Samuel Langhorne Clemens (Mark Twain's given name), does not hide behind the lectern, but stands free of the podium, indeed, walking back and forth, moving animatedly during the lecture. He begins with an apology. He was just in Dresden, giving a lecture for a worthy cause, when the deacon stormed up to him and demanded, "Sir, where are your white kid gloves? How do you expect to read without white kid gloves?"

"I didn't know what to say, so I said, 'I generally read with my glasses.'" To which the other replied, "There are three sacred customs in Germany, which are not to be violated: toasting the Emperor, conveying dinner blessings after a meal, and wearing white gloves while lecturing."

"Because I'm breaking one of these three cardinal rules of good manners once again, I feel ashamed to appear before a German auditorium filled with American citizens," Mr. Clemens confessed with remorse. Never, except perhaps at Julius Stettenheim's dinner speeches, have I ever heard such roaring laughter, as that which broke out after every sentence. Mark Twain speaks dryly, seriously, supporting his speech with gestures, but never smiling. Indeed, not even his eyes laugh. What he says sounds improvised. He read only a few passages from his book, "The Awful German Language," but everything else was spoken freely, in a conversational tone, as if it were a work in progress.

His comments on the German language are irresistibly funny—about separable prefixes, for example *das Abreisen* (departure), in which one says so much between the *Ab* and the *reisen*, that one is sure to miss the train; about those treacherous datives, whose plurals sound so odd that someone could mistake a dative dog for twins; and especially about word genders. That a wench is sexless, along with a lass, is truly a little harsh, grammatically, for those poor things, and he doesn't find it all that pleasant that sometimes a man's head is a male *Kopf* and sometimes a neutral *Haupt*. Of course, the abundance of genders for people, places, and things affects the language, and so he attempted to carry over this diversity to his language, too, by telling a little story equipped with the correct forms of "he," "she," and "it."

To fully appreciate the comedy of the *Tale of the Fishwife*, one requires a Yankee's ear. After a pretty young American woman played a familiar cantilena and an allegro by Goltermann on a cello, Mark Twain told the story of the Blue Jay from his *Tramp Abroad*. At the end of the evening, he delighted his audience with an account of a dialogue with his first interviewer, when he so utterly disappointed the man thirsting for knowledge that he—Mark Twain—was advised, for God's sake, to hermetically seal his mouth if he didn't want to thoroughly lose his reputation. He had so soundly duped the interviewer. The humor of this scene was truly American and bordered on strange.

Despite this method of deterrence, I fear German interviewers won't stay away from Mr. Clemens after tonight. He has settled in here for the winter, with his wife and his two pretty, grown-up daughters; they say that he's the Berlin correspondent for a big New York paper. It will be particularly interesting to see how our life and our circumstances are reflected in that sharply satiric yet charmingly humorous head of his. Mark Twain spoke only of our language and our white kid gloves today. What will it be like if he tells us, with gloves off, what he really thinks of us? We've already read Hungarian, Italian, French, and Dutch descriptions of Berlin, but Mark Twain's accounts of Berlin customs, so far, have been lacking.

—G. v. Beaulieu

About Andreas Austilat:

Andreas Austilat is the deputy editor of the Sunday supplement of *Der Tagesspiegel*, Berlin's leading daily, where he has worked since 1987. He interviewed many celebrities—such as Rosanne Cash (daughter of Johnny Cash), architect David Chipperfield, fashion designer Tommy Hilfinger, as well as authors Ian Kershaw and Kathy Reichs—, and also the last survivors of the gigantic airship "Hindenburg," which crashed in 1937 in Lakehurst, New Jersey, after its transatlantic journey. He also discovered the lost copies of the oldest existing Titanic movie filmed in 1912, the year of the Titanic disaster; it was hidden in a Berlin archive. He published three travel and culture guides about Brandenburg and a history book about Zehlendorf, an affluent Berlin suburb. Austilat was born in Berlin, where he lives with his wife, his two children—a boy and a girl—and their dog Duffy. He studied history at the Free University and at first wanted to become a teacher, but decided switch to journalism early on.

About Lewis Lapham:

Lewis H. Lapham, born 1935, is an American writer. He was the editor of the American monthly *Harper's Magazine* from 1976 until 1981, and from 1983 until 2006. He is also the founder of *Lapham's Quarterly*, and has written more than a dozen books on politics and current affairs. His writing has appeared in *The American Conservative, Life, Commentary, Vanity Fair, National Review, Yale Literary Magazine, ELLE, Fortune, Forbes, American Spectator, The New York Times, The Walrus, Maclean's, The Observer* (London), and the *Wall Street Journal*. Lapham also served as a judge for the PEN/Newman's Own First Amendment Award. In addition, Lapham is the host and author of the PBS series, *America's Century* as well as the host of *The World in Time*: radio discussions with scholars and historians on Bloomberg Radio. He is also on the Board of Trustees of the Advisory Council of the Mark Twain House in Hartford, Connecticut.

About Sources

Mark Twain's journey to Berlin has never been fully researched; and the number of sources is limited. Twain himself left his diary, but it is rather sketchy. Due to his rheumatism, most of his notes consist of a few words only, sometimes even misspelled. Also, quite a few entries have evidently been made weeks, if not months afte the event. The diary as well as numerous letters from and to Twain are with the Mark Twain Papers in Berkeley. We left the spelling, but added additional letters in parenthesis, if necessary. We also used the memories Twain dictated to Albert Bigelow Paine for his official biography (as well as the biography itself). This, however, happened only in 1907, and Berlin was mentioned sparsely.

The second important source is Henry William Fisher's book *Abroad with Mark Twain and Eugene Fields*. Fisher, however, should be treated with caution. While he claims to have spend a lot of time with Twain, Twain himself rarely mentions stories Fisher attributes to him. Also, Fisher published his book after a wave of anti-German sentiment in America in World War I, while Twain himself was Germanophile, so this should be taken with a grain of salt. Another source is James Dickie's book *In the Kaiser's Capital*. Dickie, however, has only met Twain later in New York. Twain's daughter Clara has left memories, and there is also an (unpublished) diary of the youngest daughter, Jean. But Clara's memories are flawed. She remembers, for instance, that her father left Berlin for a longer period of time to go back to New York. Given the many appointments he had in the city at that time, this is impossible.

Twain spent a lot of his time in Berlin with American ex-pats as well as with German officials, most remarkably Rudolf Lindau, Bismarck's worldly press secretary, who was also a travel writer and a novelist. Those two must have had fascinating conversations, but practically nothing is recorded. The same can be said about Twain's conversations with Maximilian von Versen, Fritz von Rottenburg, and other Germans. Twain surely had an opinion about the political situation in 1890s Berlin, but sadly, he never published it, so we are left with guesswork.

Sources

Original Stories by Mark Twain

- Mark Twain. [*The Berlin Postal Service*], 18 January 1892, Microfilm Edition of Mark Twain's Literary Manuscripts Available in the Mark Twain Papers, The Bancroft Library, University of California, Berkeley.
- Mark Twain. *The Chicago of Europe*. In: *The Chicago Daily Tribnue*, April 3, 1892, page 33.
- Mark Twain. *Conversations with Satan* (excerpt) in: Twenty-Two Easy Pieces by Mark Twain: Unpublished Manuscripts Selected from the Mark Twain Papers (2001), © Bancroft Library, Berkeley, CA, University of California Press.
- Mark Twain. [*Fragment of Prussian History. Wilhelmina, Margravine of Bayreuth*], 1897-1898. Microfilm Edition of Mark Twain's Literary Manuscripts Available in the Mark Twain Papers, The Bancroft Library, University of California, Berkeley.
- Mark Twain. *The Innocents Abroad*. Penguin Classics, New York, NY, 2007. Originally published in 1867 by American Publishing Co.
- Mark Twain. [*On Renting A Flat in Berlin*], 1891. Partly Published in: Paine, Albert Bigelow. *Mark Twain, Biography*: New York, Harper & Bros., 1912. Full text at the Microfilm Edition of Mark Twain's Literary Manuscripts. Available in the Mark Twain Papers, The Bancroft Library, University of California, Berkeley.
- Mark Twain. *A Tramp Abroad*. Penguin Classics, New York, NY, 1997. Originally Published in 1880 by American Publishing Company. Appendix D: "The Awful German Language."

Sources from the Mark Twain Papers, The Bancroft Library, University of California, Berkeley

- Clemens, Jean. Diary October 1891–August 1892 (unpubl.).
- Letters from Mark Twain and Olivia Clemens to various recipients from October 1891 to April 1891.
- Mark Twain. Mark Twain's autobiographical dictations according to Albert Bigelow Paine (1907).
- Mark Twain. Notebook 31 August 1891-July 1892, No. 31.
- Various letters to Mark Twain from October 1891 to April 1891.

Mark Twain's notebooks, autobiographical dictations, and letters are all published in Microfilm Edition of Mark Twain's Literary Manuscripts. Available in the Mark Twain Papers, The Bancroft Library, University of California, Berkeley; Microfilm Edition of Mark Twain's Manuscript Letters. Now in the Mark Twain Papers, The Bancroft Library University of California, Berkeley; or Microfilm Edition of Mark Twain's Previously Unpublished Letters.

Books

- Baedeker, Karl. *Berlin und Umgebung.* Leipzig: Baedeker, 1892.
- Clemens, Clara. *My Father, Mark Twain.* Harpers & Bros., New York, NY, 1931.
- Dickie, James F. *In the Kaiser's Capital.* University of California Press, 1910.
- Fisher, Henry W. *Abroad with Mark Twain and Eugene Fields. Tales Told by a Fellow Correspondent.* Nicholas L. Brown, New York, NY., 1922.
- Hillenbrand, Rainer (editor). *Das erzählerische Werk Rudolf Lindaus.* Peter Lang, Frankfurt/Main, 2005.
- Hillenbrand, Rainer (editor). *Die politische und literarische Korrespondenz Rudolf Lindaus.* Peter Lang, Frankfurt/Main, 2007.
- Hoffmann, Heinrich. *Slovenly Peter* (Der Struwwelpeter). Translated by Mark Twain. Harper & Bros., New York, NY, 1936.
- Klein, Hans-Günter. *Die Familie Mendelssohn:* Stammbaum von Moses Mendelssohn bis zur siebenten Generation. Zusammengestellt auf der Grundlage der Erhebung von Richard Wolff. - 2., korr. und erw. Aufl., Berlin 2007, Beiträge aus der Staatsbibliothek zu Berlin - Preußischer Kulturbesitz.
- Locher, Albert. *Mit Mark Twain durch Europa: S. L. Clemens in der Alten Welt (1891-1904).* Books on Demand, 2007.
- Löschburg, Winfried. *Unter den Linden. Geschichte einer berühmten Straße.* Der Morgen. Berlin, 1980.
- King, Grace. *Memories of a Southern Woman of Letters.* Pelican Publishing 2008, Originally published in 1932.
- Mann, Heinrich. *Der Untertan* (The Loyal Subject). Kurt Wolff, Leipzig, 1918.
- Paine, Albert Bigelow. *Mark Twain, Biography: The Personal and Literary Life of Samuel Langhorne Clemens.* Harper&Bros., New York, 1912.
- Paine, Albert Bigelow. *Mark Twain's Notebook.* Harper Row, New York, NY, 1935.

- Rodney, Robert. *Mark Twain Overseas. A Biographical Account of His Voyages, Travels, and Reception in Foreign Lands, 1866-1910*, Passeggiata Press, Pueblo, CO, 1993.
- Stiftung Deutsches Adelsarchiv. *Genealogisches Handbuch des Deutschen Adels*. Starke Verlag, Limburg, 1951.
- Werthern, Alfred von. *General von Versen: Ein Miliärisches Zeit- und Lebensbild aus hinterlassenen Briefen und Aufzeichnungen zusammengestellt*. Print on Demand, 2010.
- Winteroll, Michael. *Die Geschichte Berlins: Ein Stadtführer durch die Jahrhunderte*. Nicolai, Berlin, 2007.

Newspaper Stories

- Beaulieu, G. v.: "Amerika in Berlin." In: *Berliner Tageblatt*, Berlin, January 14, 1892.
- *Breslauer Morgen-Zeitung*: "Mark Twain." November 24, 1891.
- *Chicago Daily Tribune*: "Ate Turkey Abroad." November 27, 1891.
- Eaton, Anne T: "Mark Twain's Version of *Slovenly Peter*." In: *The New York Times*, November 17, 1935.
- Horwitz, Max: "Mark Twain in Berlin." In: *National-Zeitung*, Berlin, November 15, 1891.
- *The New York Times*: "The Start for Germany." April 12, 1878.
- *The New York Times*. "Court Calls in Berlin." January 2, 1892.
- *The New York Times*: "A Reformer of German." August 17, 1892.
- *The New York Times*: "Twain's Daughter Talks About Him." June 14, 1908
- *The New York Times*: "Gen. Bingham Dies at Summer Home." September 7, 1934
- *The New York Times*: "Brilliant Season at Height in Berlin." February 12, 1911
- *The New York Times:* "Miss Clemens to wed Mr. Gabrilowitsch." October 7, 1909
- *The New York Times*: "Berlin Galleries' Newest Home." Aug. 26, 2011

Sources from Berlin Archives

- Bauakte des Hauses Körnerstraße 7 1867-1902 (building record of 7 Körnerstrasse), Landesarchiv Berlin.
- Hobrechtplan 1867; Stadtplan von 1888 at
- http://www.zlb.de/berlin_studien/digitalisate/digitalisate_zbs
- Berliner Adressbücher: adressbuch.zlb.de.

Pictures

Page 14: A.F. Bradley, Bancroft Library, Bain News Service, steamboattimes.com
Page 18: Gascogne: Postcard; Taylor: Library of Congress
Page 21: Brandenburg Gate/Unter den Linden: Landesarchiv Berlin
Page 22: Körnerstrasse: Eva C. Schweitzer
Pages 24/25: Blueprint of Körnerstrasse: Landesarchiv Berlin
Page 28: Phelps/Bingham: Library of Congress;
Page 29: Office building at 66 Mohrenstrasse: Eva C. Schweitzer
Page 30: Kaiserhof: Landesarchiv Berlin
Page 31: North Korean Embassy: Eva C. Schweitzer
Page 33: Bismarck Memorial: Eva C. Schweitzer
Page 34: Kaiser Wilhelm II: Landesarchiv Berlin
Page 36: Mauerstrasse (old): Landesarchiv Berlin
Page 37: Mauerstrasse (new): Eva C. Schweitzer
Page 38: Von Versen: Werthern; Virchow, Landesarchiv Berlin
Page 39: Helmholtz, Mommsen; Landesarchiv Berlin
Page 52: Körnerstrasse today, plaque: Eva C. Schweitzer
Page 54: American Church (old): Courtesy American Church in Berlin
Page 55: American Church (new): Eva C. Schweitzer
Pages 60/61: Horse-drawn cars: Landesarchiv Berlin
Page 62: Nollendorfplatz: Landesarchiv Berlin
Page 63: Moszkowski/Willard: Public Domain
Page 68: Coca Cola store at Mohrenstrasse: Eva C. Schweitzer
Page 69: Gendarmenmarkt: Landesarchiv Berlin
Page 72: Mendelssohn building: Eva C. Schweitzer
Page 73: Mendelssohn grave; Du Bois grave: Eva C. Schweitzer
Page 74: Lindau: Bundesarchiv
Page 75: Potsdamer Strasse: Landesarchiv Berlin
Page 80: Slovenly Peter: Public Domain
Page 83: Letter. Source: Mark Twain Papers at Berkeley, CA
Page 84: Tiled stove: Eva C. Schweitzer
Page 88: Hotel Royal: Postcard from 1900
Page 89: Unter den Linden/Wilhelmstrasse: Eva C. Schweitzer
Page 90: Brandenburg Gate: Postcard from 1900 (insert: Eva C. Schweitzer)
Page 91: Brandenburg Gate: Eva C. Schweitzer
Page 92: Advertisement Bristol. Found in: National-Zeitung
Page 93: Statue Frederick the Great: Eva C. Schweitzer
Page 96: Former Royal Library: Eva C. Schweitzer
Page 97: Schopenhauer: Public Domain
Page 99: Postmuseum: Eva C. Schweitzer.
Page 102: Wilhelmstrasse: Postcard from 1900
Page 103: Wilhelmstrasse today: Eva C. Schweitzer
Page 106: Wilhelmine of Preussen: Wikimedia Commons
Page 118: Emperor Wilhelm: Landesarchiv Berlin
Page 119: Mark Twain: Public Domain
Page 124: Berlin castle: Landesarchiv Berlin,
Page 125: Castle ruins: Eva C. Schweitzer
Page 127: Street signs: Eva C. Schweitzer
Page 130: Miriam von Versen: Eva C. Schweitzer

Index

Andersen, Hans Christian: 56
Beaulieu, Gertraut Chales de: 102, 103, 161
Bernhard of Sachsen–Meiningen: 126
Bigelow, Poultney: 31, 35, 120
Bingham, Theodore: 28, 29, 64, 71
Bismarck, Herbert von: 76
Bismarck, Otto von: 15, 17, 28, 30, 31, 32, 33, 35, 38, 74, 76, 127, 163
Blackwood, William & John: 76
Bleichröder, Gerson von: 76
Boetticher, Heinrich von: 117, 157
Buffalo Bill (William Frederick Cody): 40, 100, 137
Bunsen, Berta von: 35
Bunsen, Georg von: 32, 35
Burstell, Baron von: 109
Caprivi, Leo von: 32, 117, 120, 122
Charlotte, Duchess of Preußen: 126
Chatto & Windus: 27, 58, 101, 119
Clemens, Clara: 14, 15, 16, 17, 19, 40, 50, 55, 56, 61, 62, 63, 64, 81, 90, 92, 93, 126, 128, 163
Clemens, Eliza: 35
Clemens, James; 35
Clemens, Jean: 14, 15, 16, 19, 27, 41, 91, 117, 120, 123, 126, 128, 163
Clemens, Olivia (Livy): 14, 15, 17, 19, 26, 41, 63, 65, 71, 72, 77, 79, 89, 93, 101, 105, 106, 116, 126, 128
Clemens, Susy: 14, 15, 17, 19, 61, 62, 64, 72, 92, 126, 128
Coleman, Chapman: 71, 89, 123, 126
Crane, Susan: 15, 19, 41, 93
Deutsche Verlags-Anstalt: 101
DeVoto, Bernard: 10
Dickens, Charles: 155
Dickie, James: 27, 53, 54, 65, 66, 78, 79, 101, 163
Dietrich, Marlene: 23, 124
Dobenek, Herr von: 111
Du Bois-Reymond, Alard (also spelled as Raymond): 71, 72
Du Bois-Reymond, Emil: 72, 73
Emerson, Ralph Waldo: 11
Engel, H.: 105
Fischer, S.: 23
Fischer, Vic: 56, 129
Fisher, Henry William: 29, 30, 32, 35, 40, 41, 65, 68, 78, 81, 82, 91, 95, 96, 104, 105, 106, 163
Fontane, Theodor: 23, 50, 76
Franklin, Benjamin: 57
Frederick the Great, King of Preußen: 15, 93, 94, 95, 106
Frederick Wilhelm I, King of Preußen: 13
Fritz, the porter: 65-67, 83
Gabrilowitsch, Ossip: 128
Goethe, Johann Wolfgang von: 65
Grant, Ulysses S.: 11, 20, 156
Habberton, John: 147, 148
Hall, Frederick: 26, 27, 31, 55, 56, 70, 71, 79, 81, 83, 101, 118
Halstead, Murat: 19, 90
Harris, Joel Chandler: 71
Harrison, Benjamin: 27
Harte, Bret: 147, 148
Heine, Heinrich: 59, 157
Helmholtz, Anna von: 73
Helmholtz, Hermann von: 38, 39, 73, 116, 127, 141, 142, 143, 145
Henderson, Ernest Flagg: 35
Henry, Margrave of Bayreuth: 108, 113, 114, 115
Henry, Prince of Preußen: 31, 120, 128-129
Hensel, Fanny: 72, 73
Hensel, Lili: 72
Hensel, Sebastian: 71, 72, 74
Hessling, Diederich: 124, 125
Hewitt, Peter Cooper: 129
Hobrecht, James: 50
Hoffmann, Heinrich: 56
Holmes, Oliver Wendell: 11
Horwitz, Max: 57, 58, 78, 119, 147-153
Isherwood, Christopher: 61
Jackson, John: 90, 126
Joan of Arc: 126, 128
Kalisch, David: 118
Kant, Immanuel: 95
Killisch, Rittmeister: 50, 83
King, Grace: 104
Köppe, Ernst: 93

Index

Labouchère, Henry du Pré: 30, 56
Langdon, Charles: 79
Langdon, family: 77
Leary, Katie: 19, 53
Leo VIII, Pope: 20
Liebermann, Max: 13
Lilienthal, Otto: 16
Lindau, Rudolf: 74, 75, 76, 77, 81, 120, 126, 128, 131, 163
Litfass, Ernst: 100
Locher, Albert: 78, 93, 104, 105
Luther, Martin: 53
Lutz, Robert: 56
Louis XIV, King of France: 114
Mann, Heinrich: 124
Mann, Thomas: 124
McClure, Samuel Sidney: 20
McClure Syndicate: 20, 26, 56, 71, 79, 118
Mendelssohn-Bartholdy, Ernst von: 74
Mendelssohn-Bartholdy, Felix: 72, 73, 127
Mendelssohn, family: 72, 73, 74
Mendelssohn, Moses: 71, 74
Mommsen, Theodor: 39, 40, 73, 126, 127, 144, 145
Mommsen, Theodor Ernst: 40
Moszkowski, Moritz: 63, 128
Mozart, Wolfgang Amadeus: 65
Nelson, Elisabeth: 74
Nelson, Heinrich: 74
Nelson, Leonard: 74
Orthmann, Friedrich Wilhelm: 101
Paige, James: 19, 27
Paine, Albert Bigelow: 19, 26, 40, 51, 56, 64, 66, 77, 82, 104, 120, 129, 163
Palmer, Bertha: 123
Palmer, Potter: 123
Phelps, Marian: 29, 30, 71, 126
Phelps, Phelps: 30
Phelps, William Walter: 27, 28, 29, 71, 77, 81, 89, 126, 157
Porten, Henny: 41
Prächtel, Mr, "Mr. P.": 40, 42-49, 83
Pulitzer, Joseph: 30
Pulitzer, Ralf: 129
Radolin, Prince Hugo von: 120
Random House: 101
Reitzenstein, Baron von: 109
Ridder, Hermann: 129
Rockefeller, John D.: 102
Rodney, Robert M.: 57
Roosevelt, Theodore: 11
Rottenburg, Franz Johannes von: 30, 71, 121, 123, 157, 163
Rowohlt: 23
Saveur, Lambert: 104
Schauffler, Robert Haven: 129
Schiff, Jacob: 129
Schopenhauer, Arthur: 15, 95, 96, 97, 105, 127
Schurz, Carl: 129
Schwatlo, Carl: 99
Stedman, Edmund Clarence: 79
Stettenheim, Julius: 160
Strindberg, Johan August: 96
Stuckenberg, John Henry: 101, 159, 160
Sudermann, Hermann: 50, 76
Taylor, Bayard: 17, 18, 19, 104
Tower, Charlemagne: 129
Varnhagen, Rahel: 36
Versen, Alice von: 35, 36, 116
Versen, Elizabeth Alice von: 36
Versen, family: 36, 64, 89, 105, 119, 120, 121, 123, 126, 131
Versen, Hulda von: 36
Versen, Maximilian von: 35, 36, 37, 38, 119, 126, 131, 163
Versen, Miriam von: 130, 131
Victoria, Queen of England: 11, 121
Virchow, Rudolf: 37, 38, 39, 40, 127, 140, 141, 142, 143, 145
Voltaire, Francois: 95
Warner, George H.: 71, 72
Webster & Co.: 20, 26, 27, 79, 101
Webster, Charles: 26, 79
Wermuth, Adolf: 123
Wenske, Mally: 35
Werner, Anton von: 23, 50
Wilhelm II, Kaiser of Germany: 12, 15, 31, 32, 34, 35, 66, 67, 90, 91, 116, 117, 118, 120, 121, 122, 123, 125, 126, 129, 131
Wilhelmine, Margravine of Bayreuth: 15, 106, 107-115
Willard, Mary Bannister: 61, 62, 63, 81, 126
Whitmore, Franklin G.: 26, 27, 70
Whitmore, Harriet: 41

169

Berlinica Presents

2010–2013 Program

BOOK, MOVIES, AND MUSIC FROM BERLIN

JEWS IN BERLIN, by Andreas Nachama, Julius H. Schoeps, and Hermann Simon: This richly illustrated book depicts 750 years of Jewish history as well as Jewish life in Berlin today. Berlin was the center of Jewish life in Germany. Its Jewish citizens influenced the city's cultural and literary life. However, hyper-inflation, and the economic crisis provided rich soil for anti-Semitism, and this ultimately led to the Holocaust. But today, Jewish culture is flourishing once again.

Softcover, 310 pages, 6.69" x 9.61"
ISBN: 978-1-935902-60-7; $23.95

TUCHOLSKY'S BERLIN! BERLIN! shines a light on the Weimar Republic and the Golden Twenties, on the cabarets and theaters, the city and its denizens, politics and street fights, and the post-war struggle between the militaristic Right and the pacifistic Left, which foreshadowed the Third Reich. This book focuses on Tucholsky's news stories and poems about his home town; a glimpse of the age that shaped the century. This collection of stories has never been published in America.

Hardcover, 6.14" x 9.21", 198 pages, $22.95
Softcover, 5.5" x 8.5", 198 pages, $14.95
ISBN: 978-1-93590-21-8 / 20-1

ROCKING THE WALL, by Erik Kirschbaum, is about a Bruce Springsteen concert in East Berlin on July 19, 1988, that changed the world. With behind-the-scenes details, fan interviews, newspaper clippings, and Stasi files, this book takes you to a journey with Springsteen through the divided city and to the concert grounds where The Boss, live on stage, delivered a speech against the Wall.

Hardcover, 5.5" x 8.5", 142 pages, $19.95
Softcover, 5.5" x 8.5", 142 pages, $11.95
ISBN: 978-1-935902-73-7 / 74-4. Also as ebook.

WINGS OF DESIRE, by Lothar Heinke, is a whimsical, full-color picture book full of angels: angels on top of church steeples, cemeteries, on rooftops, above entrances, and in public places, angels that are really greek goddesses, and angels that are a little naughty. Some are well known, others hidden. The gift for everyone who loves Berlin.

Hardcover, 102 color pages, 7" x 10"
ISBN: 978-1-935902-14-0; $25.95
Softcover, 102 color pages, 7" x 10"
ISBN: 978-1-935902-18-8; $18.95

BERLIN FOR FREE, by Monika Märtens, is an invaluable guide to everything free in Berlin: pop, classical music, concerts in the park, art shows and exhibitions, museums and movies, readings and theater, sports events, city tours, gay life, and street fairs for kids as well as grown-ups. The book includes hundreds of addresses, phone numbers, and web sites. All information is fact-checked and recently updated.

Softcover, 104 pages, 5" x 8"
ISBN: 978-1-935902-50-9; $11.95

THE BERLIN COOKBOOK, by Rose Marie Donhauser, reveals how to make schnitzel, currywurst, and those jelly donuts known as Berliners. But it also talks about Berlin food: how the "Eisbein" got its name, why Friedrich the Great forced Prussian farmers to plant potatoes, that meatballs were imported by French Huguenots, and many more stories.

Hardcover, 8.5" x 10", 98 pages, $24.95,
Softcover, 8.5" x 8.5", 98 pages, $19.95
ISBN: 978-1-935902-51-5 / 50-8

WALLFLOWER by Holly-Jane Rahlens, is four hours in the life of Molly Lenzfeld, a sixteen-year-old New Yorker in Berlin. It's Thanksgiving 1989, two weeks after the fall of the Wall. Molly, the daughter of a German-Jewish mother who fled the Nazis in 1938, is off to her mother's birth house in East Berlin. On the subway, she meets Eastern wildflower Mick Maier. For both, it's love at first sight—and a journey into Berlin's underground.

Softcover, 150 pages, 5.5" x 8.5"
ISBN: 978-1-935902-70-6; $11.95

BERLIN 1945 shows a city in ruins, a heartwrenching account of the devastation of after World War II. But it is also a testimony of how families survived after the Nazis fell. These 200 black-and-white photos from the archives of the daily *Berliner Kurier* were taken by Red Army soldiers in 1945, when Soviet forces occupied Berlin. These pictures have never been shown to an American audience before.

Hardcover, 8.5"x11", 150 pages, $23.95
Softcover 7.44" x 9.69", 150 pages, $17.95
ISBN: 978-1-935902-03-4 / 02-7

THE BERLIN WALL TODAY, by Michael Cramer, is a richly illustrated, full-color book about the remnants of the Wall. It tells about struggle, survival, rebirth, and what is happening today, at places like the party hotspot Wall Park, the Museum of Forbidden Art, the *East Side Gallery,* and Checkpoint Charlie.

Softcover, 86 pages, 123 pictures, 14 maps, dimensions: 8.5" x 8.5"
ISBN: 978-1935902-102; $15.95

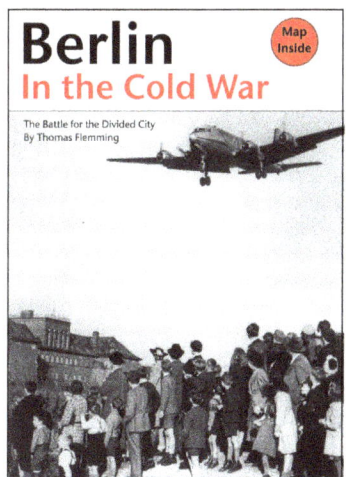

BERLIN IN THE COLD WAR, by Thomas Flemming, describes the conflict between the United States and the Soviets as it played out in the divided city that was frontier town, spy post, and battlefield. It highlights the dramatic events that affected the whole world: the blockade of 1948 and the airlift, the June 1953 uprising against the Communists, stories of escape and espionage, and the fall of the Iron Curtain. Includes many pictures and a map.

Softcover, 90 pages, 6.96" x 9.61"
ISBN: 978-1-935902-80-5; $10.95

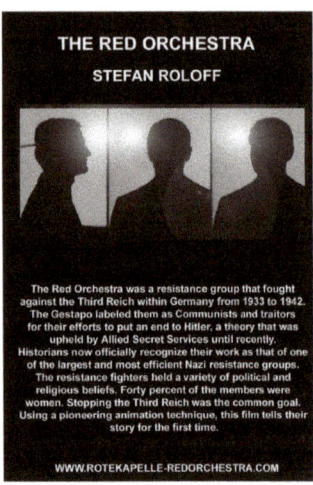

THE PATH TO NUCLEAR FISSION, by Rosemarie Reed, is about a brilliant Jewish scientist, Lise Meitner, whose inventions led to the atomic bomb—to her own great horror. In 1907, the shy student Meitner met Otto Hahn in Berlin, with whom she later discovered nuclear fission. Hahn helped Meitner to flee the Nazis, but he didn't credit her when he was awarded the Nobel Prize. Narrated by Linda Hunt.

Language English/German (subtitled), run time: 81:00, $19.95 at Amazon

THE RED ORCHESTRA was a Berlin-based resistance group that fought the Third Reich. The Gestapo labeled them Communists, and so did the Allied Secret Services. Only recently were they recognized by historians. This documentary, made by Stefan Roloff, the son of a survivor, tells their story for the first time to an American audience, using a pioneering technique and powerful original footage.

Language English/German (subtitled), run time: 56:47, $24.95 at Amazon

BERLIN, MON AMOUR, by Adrienne Haan is a tribute to 1920s Germany. It contains sixteen songs, mostly by Kurt Weill and Friedrich Hollaender, among them classics like "Pirate Jenny" and "Falling in Love Again." The album is arranged for Big Band, conveying a Broadway feeling that makes the soul swing.

Audio CD, in English or German, 48 minutes, $15.95 at Amazon

www.ingramcontent.com/pod-product-compliance
Lightning Source LLC
Chambersburg PA
CBHW041308240426
43661CB00037B/1464/J